Made Free

Workbook

Embrace a Life Lived in Freedom

© 2020 by Tracy L. Edwards

Publisher information

All rights reserved. No part of this publication may be reproduced, stored in a retrieval system, or transmitted in any form or by any means—for example, electronic, photocopy, recording—without the prior written permission of Tracy L. Edwards. The only exception is brief quotations in printed reviews.

Library of Congress Cataloging-in-Publication Data

Edwards, Tracy L., 1966–

    Made Free Workbook : Embrace a Life Lived in Freedom

    ISBN 978-1-7355944-2-2

All scripture quotations, unless otherwise indicated, are taken from the New King James Version®. Copyright © 1982 by Thomas Nelson, Inc. Used by permission. All rights reserved.

Scripture quotations marked (NIV) are taken from the Holy Bible, New International Version®, NIV®. Copyright © 1973, 1978, 1984 by Biblica, Inc.™ Used by permission of Zondervan. All rights reserved worldwide. www.zondervan.com

Scripture quotations marked (The Message) are taken from *THE MESSAGE*. Copyright © by Eugene H. Peterson 1993, 1994, 1995, 1996, 2000, 2001, 2002. Used by permission of NavPress Publishing Group.

Scripture quotations taken from the Amplified® Bible (AMP), Copyright © 2015 by The Lockman Foundation Used by permission. www.Lockman.org

Dedication

To the One who made me free, Almighty God. My life is Yours.

To my husband Steve, I love you. You are my safe place.

To my children and grandchildren, you make me proud.

To the staff at Freedom Church, you make my heart happy.

Contents

Introduction 01

Part 1—Laying the Foundation 03

    Session 1—The Heart of the Father 05

    Session 2—Jesus Christ, Redeemer 13

    Session 3—The Holy Spirit, Spirit of Truth 21

Part 2—Reality Check: Work is Required 31

    Session 4—New Creation in Christ 39

    Session 5—Kingdom Mindset 51

    Session 6—Yoke of Bondage 61

    Session 7—Lies We Believe 83

    Session 8—Planted 93

    Session 9—Gifted and Positioned by God 101

    Session 10—Weapons of our Warfare 111

    Session 11—Prayer Is Not Optional 121

    Session 12—Pressing Toward the Goal 131

Part 3—Final Encouragement 137

Acknowledgments 138

About the Author 139

"Heavenly Father, through Your grace, goodness and mercy, You have made a way for me to be made free. Thank You for loving me so much, You sent Your Son, Jesus Christ to redeem me. Thank You for sending Your Holy Spirit to be my Teacher, Helper and Comfort. I pray that as I go through this workbook, my heart and mind will be transformed, and I will live in the freedom Christ has given me. May my journey give You glory, in Jesus' Name I pray. Amen."

Introduction

The book and this workbook wasn't written to be a quick and easy read. It is my hope that as you read through it, you'll take the necessary time to process through the principles so you can continually be made free by the goodness of God.

You are so courageous to begin this journey, even if you have doubts and maybe a little bit of fear. God loves you and He is with you through every step. His passion is to see you fulfill the thoughts He has for you, thoughts of peace, to give you a hope and a future greater than you know.

You will struggle with some of the things written in the book and some of the questions asked in this workbook. Don't stop! Trust the Holy Spirit to lead you through and set you free from the things hindering your life from the fullness God desires for you.

You will have to face some difficult things, about yourself and others. Trust that Jesus Christ will never leave nor forsake you. He is with you every step of the way. Don't give up, keep pursuing the freedom that can only be found in Christ.

God desires you to live a life in peace, joy, love, and fulfillment. So, work through the questions. Don't rush, really think about the questions. Write down your thoughts, even the hard ones, so healing and restoration can take place.

So, go get your Bible.

You'll need it as you go through this workbook. Some of the verses I write out, others I do not. This is to help you get comfortable going to the Word of God. The Word of God has the answer for every situation you face. So, keep your Bible and a journal handy. There are places to write out your answers and thoughts. But there may be times when you need more space to write what is revealed to you.

Let's get started on the road to be Made Free!

In Him I Live,

Tracy Edwards

Up-Word@outlook.com

PART ONE

Made Free Workbook

Laying the Foundation

Foundations are important. Jesus teaches about the consequences of building your life upon a solid foundation or upon shifting sand.

> *"Therefore whoever hears these sayings of Mine, and does them, I will liken him to a wise man who built his house on the rock: and the rain descended, the floods came, and the winds blew and beat on that house; and it did not fall, for it was founded on the rock.*
>
> *"But everyone who hears these sayings of Mine, and does not do them, will be like a foolish man who built his house on the sand: and the rain descended, the floods came, and the winds blew and beat on that house; and it fell. And great was its fall."* (Matthew 7:24-27)

Our lives were meant to be built on the solid foundation of the principles of God. Every other foundation will not stand.

Because many of us have foundations which are not solid and based on Truth, God takes us through a process to tear down anything that is not of Him and damaging to us. Then, He builds us up on the Rock so that when life events happen, we are not destroyed.

Please do not be deceived that you will only have to go through foundational repairs or maintenance once. It's a lifelong process, but it does get easier each round. God's restoration process usually goes in layers. One layer of hurt, incorrect belief, and correction at a time. It's, I believe, a protective measure for us. But there will be times when He uses the same situation, or type of situation, to reveal something more.

His growth process to get us to maturity in our freedom in Christ sometimes is mistaken for, "we didn't get it right the first time." It's not about getting it right, it is about continual healing, restoration, and then being entrusted with greater things, for His glory and our good.

As we experience more and more freedom in Christ, when He takes us back to our past, to learn, not live there again, we can see things from a healthier, healed perspective. Rather than the distorted lens of youth, lack of understanding, pain, and/or self-preservation.

Incorporate foundation checks in your life-long journey with the Lord.

You were made to be free.

Session 1

Made Free Workbook

The Heart of the Father

"He who does not love does not know God, for God is love." (1 John 4:8)

God, since the beginning of time, has revealed Himself to His creations—human beings. God created us, male and female, in His image. And, He created us out of a heart of deep love and a desire to be in continual fellowship and relationship with us.

It can be difficult for us to believe God is love. And, even if we do believe God is love, we often, knowingly or unknowingly, can water it down to a human experience and understanding of love. It's because we view things through our own perspectives. Our perspectives are obtained, developed and infused in us through many influences. Relationships with parents, family, friends, strangers, teachers, co-workers, and so on all contribute to our perspective regarding ourselves, relationships and the world.

Our perspectives are altered through obtaining new information and life experiences. They can become clearer through seeking Truth, or more distorted through believing lies. We'll deal with a number of these in upcoming chapters. In the meantime, we need to lay the foundation of Truth in our lives that God is love.

I also need to deal with the beautiful, yet quite messy, gift of freewill. God created us with a powerful and fathomless organ called the mind. With it, He also gave us the responsibility to think, create, solve problems and, hopefully, make healthy and wise decisions. He has given us, all of us, the ability to choose what we believe and how we live the life He has given us. He, since the beginning of time, has implored us to choose Him, to act justly, love mercy, and to walk humbly with Him. He desires us to choose life. He always guides us to love. Unfortunately, people use their freewill to deny Him and to harm others. God doesn't make them commit evil. They choose to. God will not negate the freewill He created and empowered us with.

But He ALWAYS points us to faith, hope and above all, love.

In 1 John 4:8, the word love comes from the Greek words, **agan** *(much)* and **agape** *(to love, feast of love, a dear love)*. Their meanings are rooted in the Hebrew word, **'âgab**, pronounced, **aw-gab**, which is a prim root meaning, *to breathe after, to love, to dote*.

1) Take a moment to think about the fact God is love. Think about the fact that He breathes after you and He dotes on you. Write down how this Truth makes you feel. What feeling did you experience when you read this Truth?

_____
_____
_____

2) Write down any thought you had that tried to cause doubt or to question the Truth that God is love and He dotes on you.

_____
_____
_____
_____
_____

3) Stay quiet and ask the Holy Spirit to reveal to you why you doubted or questioned God's love for you. Write down whatever word, person or image came to your mind.

_____
_____
_____
_____
_____

Perspective—defined by Noah Webster's 1828 dictionary as *"a glass through which objects are viewed."* As I mentioned earlier, our perspective of ourselves and the world is shaped by influences and experiences. We process information, people, world events through the glass, lens, in which we view them through. The lens we view things through impacts how we see ourselves, process our experiences and govern the decisions we make.

Here are several examples of how our perspective of God is shaped by internal and external influences and experiences. I encourage you to go through these thoughtfully. Some of them may be a little too close to your heart and God wants to change your perspective through new information and experience.

Think about how these statements could shape your perspective of God.
- God doesn't exist.
- You better be good or God is going to 'get' you!
- If God is love, why doesn't He stop horrible things from happening?
- God doesn't care about me. There are other more important people He needs to be concerned about.
- God can't be love, otherwise I wouldn't have been hurt like I was.
- You were hurt or abandoned by your earthly father or father-figure.
- People in the church have hurt you.
- People I care about have told me, I'm a fool for believing in God.

4) Now, write down up to ten things you think have shaped your perspective on God.

Again, don't rush. This is an opportunity to either break off lies you've been told or to gain a deeper understanding of who God is. Being honest with yourself gives you the opportunity to deal with things that may be hindering your relationship with God. And, it will give you the opportunity to receive more of what God has for you as He changes your perspective. Write down positive thoughts as well, as God will either reinforce it or deepen your revelation of them.

a. _____

b. _____

c. _____

d. _____

f. _____

g. _____

h. _____

i. _____

j. _____

k. _____

5) Of those listed, write down those that contradict or limit the Truth that God is love. How do they stand up when you process them through the fact that God is love? How does it change or expand your perspective of God?

_____
_____
_____
_____
_____
_____
_____
_____
_____
_____

Read 1 Corinthians 13:4-8a in your Bible. Doesn't your heart yearn to be loved and to love like that? It's who God is. I've taken some liberties with the verse and made a few word changes.

> *"God endures long and is patient and kind; He never is envious nor boils over with jealousy; He is not boastful or vainglorious, and does not display Himself haughtily. He is not conceited—arrogant and inflated with pride; God is not rude (unmannerly), and He does not act unbecomingly. God does not insist on His own rights or His own way, for He is not self-seeking; He is not touchy or fretful or resentful; and He takes no account of the evil done to Him—pays no attention to a suffered wrong. God does not rejoice at injustice and unrighteousness, but He rejoices when right and truth prevail. He bears up under anything and everything that comes, He is ever ready to believe the best of every person, His hopes are fadeless under all circumstances and **He endures everything** [without weakening]. Father God never fails…"* (AMP, classic edition, emphasis added)

I'd like you to take each of these lines and answer the questions beneath each one. Don't rush through the verse lines or questions. This is an opportunity to address any known or unknown distortions regarding your belief of who God is, how you see Him, yourself and the world around you. It's also a wonderful opportunity for God to change your perspective of Him, therefore, deepening your relationship with Him.

"God endures long and is patient and kind;

6) Write down a couple of examples in your life where you experienced the patience and kindness of God:
___
___
___
___

7) Describe any area of your life where you felt God wasn't patient or kind towards you:
___
___
___
___

8) Why do you feel God wasn't patient or kind in that set of circumstances?
___
___
___
___

9) Keeping in mind God is patient and kind, but also, He will not violate our or other's freewill, write down how you can see God's patience and kindness in the circumstance.
___
___
___
___

"He never is envious nor boils over with jealousy;"

10) Write down a couple of reasons why God wouldn't be envious, or needs to boil over with (negative) jealousy:
___
___
___
___

11) Exodus 34:14 says, *"For you shall worship no other god; for the Lord, Whose name is Jealous, is a jealous God."* **Write down why this is not a contradiction of 1 Corinthians 13.**

"He is not boastful or vainglorious, and does not display Himself haughtily."

12) There are many verses in the Word of God where He describes Himself and/or His creation in ways seemingly quite vainglorious. Why do you think He really isn't being boastful?

"He is not conceited—arrogant and inflated with pride;"

13) Why do you think there isn't any reason why God should be conceited or inflated with pride?

"God is not rude (unmannerly), and He does not act unbecomingly."

14) Think about a time in your life where you recognized (sensed, had the feeling, knew) God was in the midst of your circumstance. What was His behavior towards you?

"God does not insist on His own rights or His own way, for He is not self-seeking;"

15) God tells us to follow His ways, His commands. What is the difference between God 'insisting' on His rights and ways and us insisting on ours? In what ways is He not insisting on having His own way?

"He is not touchy or fretful or resentful;"

16) Why do you think some people believe God is ill-humored, angry, or resentful?

_____
_____
_____
_____

"He takes no account of the evil done to Him—pays no attention to a suffered wrong."

17) Do you believe God has a 'tab' of all the things you may have wronged Him by? Why do you believe that?

_____
_____
_____
_____

18) How does knowing He takes no account of evil done to Him change your relationship with Him when you sin?

_____
_____
_____
_____

"God does not rejoice at injustice and unrighteousness,"

19) What do you believe God feels when He sees people doing harm to others?

_____
_____
_____
_____

"He rejoices when right and truth prevail."

20) Have you experienced peace and a sense of joy when you see people being kind to others? How much more do you believe God feels the same?

_____
_____
_____
_____

"He bears up under anything and everything that comes,"

21) How does this Truth change your perspective regarding other religions and world events?

_____
_____
_____
_____

"He is ever ready to believe the best of every person,"

22) How many times have you made mistakes? And, how many times have you felt God encouraging you to return to Him, try again, or get back up?

_____
_____
_____
_____

"His hopes are fadeless under all circumstances, and..."

23) To fade means to lose strength, to disappear. How does the Truth that God's hopes are fadeless change your perspective regarding God's faithfulness about you, the world, and/or others?

_____
_____
_____
_____

"He endures everything [without weakening]."

24) How does this change your perspective on God when you doubt or question God?

_____
_____
_____
_____

25) What about when you doubt or question yourself and who you are as His child?

_____
_____
_____
_____

"Father God never fails..."

26) How does this make you feel when you experience disappointment?

_____
_____
_____
_____

God is love. This is Truth. Love is His motivator for everything He does and allows. I realize reading it and saying it are easier than believing it and living it out every day. Here is how God has worked in my life. Once I read something in His Word, or I hear or experience something that challenges my current perspective of who He is, I am, or how I process life, He begins to allow me to see His Truth regarding the situation.

I can choose to pursue the deeper revelation and allow Him to change my perspective to a clearer, truth-filled level. Or, I can choose not to. I am not going to sugarcoat it and tell you it is an easy process of allowing your mindset and heart to be changed by His Truth. It takes work. You have been and are inundated with other influences that have shaped your mindset and perspective. It will take time and effort to break those off and allow God to bring Truth. I can tell you in all sincerity, it is worth it. So, I encourage you, do the work.

27) Even if you're still struggling with the Truth God is love, how can this Truth change your perspective on:

a. Who God is: _____
_____
_____

b. Who you are: _____
_____
_____

c. Friends: _____
_____
_____

d. Strangers: _____
_____
_____

e. The world: _____
_____
_____

f. Life experiences: _____
_____
_____

g. Other notes: _____
_____
_____

Session 2

Made Free Workbook

Jesus Christ, Redeemer

"Stand fast therefore in the liberty by which Christ has made us free, and do not be entangled again with a yoke of bondage." (Galatians 5:1)

In Genesis 1:26, God makes an interesting statement, "Then God said, *"Let Us make man in Our image, according to Our likeness."* Before this, except for Genesis 1:2, no other being was mentioned. Creation was formed through the Word of God, "And God said, *"Let there be..."* And, it became so according to the Word He spoke.

Who is the "Us" God is bringing into the creation of mankind? God brought the Trinity into the creative process to create a distinctly different life than any other creature God had created. The Trinity is the Father, the Son, Jesus Christ our Redeemer, and the Holy Spirit, our Helper. We will discuss the Holy Spirit more in Chapter 3.

Why did God, for lack of a better word, consult, with Jesus Christ and the Holy Spirit to bring forth life in a different form? He was more than able to do it on His own. Remember, God is Sovereign. He is Creator. His power and authority are above all. He really didn't have to enlist help to create man. But He chose to.

God chose to bring Jesus Christ and the Holy Spirit into the creation of man because man's purpose, above all else, is to have a relationship with the Father, the Son and the Spirit. *"Let Us make man in Our image, according to Our likeness."* We are comprised of mind, body and spirit.

We were not created like any other created being or thing. Yes, there are similarities and we inhabit the same earth. But we were created in the image and according to the likeness of Father God, Jesus Christ, and the Holy Spirit. As with the Genesis account of creation, there are endless debates about whether we physically look like God, male and female attributes, etc. These debates, in my opinion, overshadow the Truth that is evident in our creation. We were created unique. We did not evolve from an amoeba or a beast.

God created mankind in HIS IMAGE and He breathed Himself into us. (Genesis 2:7) An impartation of who He is, is fused into our DNA. He created us with a mind capable of reasoning and intelligence far above any other created thing in this earth.

I have a great respect and love for all of creation. And, I believe animals have incredible intelligence and abilities. We can also learn so much from them (because God created them and how they function). But I have never heard of an ape's intelligence evolving so much it created an artificial leg. Nor, have I ever heard of an ant colony surpassing other generations of ants in their understanding of survival to plant, grow and harvest their own food.

We were created with the capacity to understand. We were given a will, the ability to choose. And, we were created with active power. God made us responsible, to have dominion, over the earth. It is our responsibility to steward the earth. And, He blessed us, *"...be fruitful and multiply, fill the earth and subdue it, have dominion..."*

We were created with the nature of God. We were created as a reflection of Him, who He is. This Truth irrevocably defines who we are. And, in that Truth, we were not meant to be separate from Him, nor carry the weight of sin, nor be entangled in its bondage.

Why is this so important? Our belief in how we were created is foundational to our identity and how we approach life. It defines how we choose to live.

What does it have to do with Jesus Christ as our Redeemer? Absolutely everything.

This, hopefully, will become increasingly evident as we work through MADE FREE!

Read Genesis Chapters 1-3.

1) How does knowing God, Jesus Christ and the Holy Spirit worked cohesively together in your creation affect how you see yourself?

_____
_____
_____
_____

2) List 5 things about yourself and then write out why you see yourself this way. Dig deep, don't write in fear of others seeing what you wrote. When no one is around, what do you really think about yourself? And, you need to know the "why" behind what you feel. Understanding the "why" behind our thoughts and feelings helps us understand who we are and why we do some of the things we do.

a. I am: _____.

Why do you think this about yourself? _____
_____
_____
_____
_____

b. I am: _____.

Why do you think this about yourself? _____
_____
_____
_____
_____

c. I am: _____.

Why do you think this about yourself? _____
_____
_____
_____
_____

d. I am: _____.

Why do you think this about yourself? _____
_____
_____
_____
_____

e. I am: _____.

Why do you think this about yourself? _____
_____
_____

3) Do you fully believe you were created in the image and likeness of God? _____

Why do you believe this way? It's important to know <u>why</u> you believe <u>what</u> you believe.

---

4) God created us the with ability to understand, to process and to provide solutions for small and complex matters.

a. How does this Truth impact how you deal with any circumstance of life?

---

b. How does this Truth effect how you deal with internal struggles?

---

5) How does knowing you were created with the nature of God imparted in you make you feel?

---

6) How does knowing you were created as a reflection of God make you feel?

---

7) How does it affect how you see yourself?

God did not create us with the knowledge to know the difference between good and evil. (Genesis 2:16-17) The enemy manipulated God's warning that man, and woman, would die to deceive them into disobeying God's one command. The enemy also appealed to their (our) lack of understanding of and security in who God had created them to be.

> *"Then the serpent said to the woman, "You will not surely die. For God knows that in the day you eat of it your eyes will be opened, and you will be like God, knowing good and evil." (Genesis 3:4-5)*

God said they would die. The enemy said they would not die. But instead of immediately rebuking what the enemy said and believing what God had told them, they continued to listen. They *entertained* thoughts that did not line up with God's Word.

Then, the enemy told them a truth, *"For God knows that in the day you eat of it your eyes will be opened."* Their eyes were opened, and the first thing they experienced was shame. (Genesis 3:7) The second was fear. (Genesis 3:10) The enemy failed to mention the price they would pay for trusting him rather than God. The enemy failed to mention how destructive and weighty shame is.

The enemy even sweetened the deal to encourage disobedience, *"...and you will be like God..."* The problem was they did not understand they were already *'like'* God. They were created with His nature, in His likeness. They were drawn away because they were tempted to become someone they can never be.

We can never be God. We are the created, not the Creator.

What justice did man deserve when he chose to dishonor God and trusted an enemy instead?

Remember, God is just, and He is holy. God had every right to destroy man right then. But God is merciful and kind.

He removed man from the Garden so man would not eat from the Tree of Life and live forever in the state his choice put him in. A state filled with shame, fear, the weight of sin and its continual bondage that binds us.

Man chose sin. He chose to live outside of, in disobedience to, God's commands.

Then, Jesus.

8) How difficult is it for you to trust God (in all situations)? _____

a. Why do you think that is?

_____
_____
_____
_____

9) How much time do you spend thinking about something that you know doesn't align with God or His Word? _____

a. Why do you think that is?

_____
_____
_____
_____

10) Overall, are you content with who God created you to be? You will know your degree of contentment by how much time you spend wishing you were like someone else, or you find yourself jealous of others, or wanting something others have. Be honest with yourself. _____
_____
_____
_____
_____

a. Why or why not?

_____
_____
_____
_____

11) Is your relationship with God all you want it to be? _____

a. Why or why not? What is causing the hinderance?

_____
_____
_____
_____

12) Do you battle with sin? _____

a. Why do you think that is?

_____
_____
_____
_____

13) Is sin holding you in bondage?

_____
_____
_____
_____

14) Why do you think sin has that strong of a hold on you?

_____
_____
_____
_____

a. Do you want to be set free from that sin?

b. Do your actions reflect your desire to be free from sin?

15) When God reveals, confronts, something in your life He is asking you to change, what is your first response and why?

God gave man the gift of freewill. He gave man the liberty to use His gift of freewill in the manner they desired. This beautiful gift, unfortunately, can be used to commit unspeakable evil. God is often blamed for the atrocities man chooses to commit.

Choices always reflect the heart of man, not necessarily the heart of God. Any heart fully committed to following the ways of the Lord will not make choices outside of God's commands, which are always rooted in love, well-being, peace, joy, respect, grace, mercy, kindness and freedom.

It is God who will administer final judgement, justice, on every man and woman. And, there will be a judgement day for us all that determines our eternity. We will be judged by God either by the standards of the Law, or by the standard of grace through Jesus Christ.

We also live this life on earth under the standards of the Law, whether people believe it or not. Or, when we choose Jesus Christ as our Redeemer, we live under the freedom of grace found in Him.

16) In what areas of your life do you struggle with a thought that begins, "If I could only do this more, or be better at, then God will….?"

17) In the depths of your being, do you think you can work your way into God's "good graces"? Why or Why not?

18) Do you think "being a good person" is enough to live a life in freedom? _____

Why or why not? _____
_____
_____
_____

There are only two ways to respond to Jesus Christ. Repentance or Rebellion.

> *Repentance,* sincere remorse; sorrow or deep contrition for sin, as an offense and dishonor to God, a violation of his holy law, and the vilest ingratitude towards a Being of infinite benevolence.

> *Rebellion*, an open and avowed renunciation of the authority of the 'government' to which one owes allegiance; open resistance to lawful authority.

Repenting for rejecting God and His ways, leads to accepting Jesus Christ as Lord over your life.

When people reject Jesus Christ, and following the commands of God, they rebel against God Himself and His redemptive plan. They will live enduring the consequences of their choice, without the grace of Jesus Christ.

19) Are you confident that Jesus Christ is your Redeemer and you have been reconciled through Him to God?
_____

20) Are you confident you will be judged by God under the grace of Jesus Christ? _____

21) Do you still engage in behavior that does not align with the commands of God? _____

Why?
_____
_____
_____
_____

Believing in Jesus Christ as your Lord and Savior does not excuse nor justify continuing to choose living outside the commands of God. You are still required to pursue living your life according to the commandments of God. Jesus said it like this,

> *"Do not think that I came to destroy the Law or the Prophets, I did not come to destroy but to fulfill... Whoever therefore breaks one of the least of these commandments, and teaches men so, shall be called least in the kingdom of heaven, but whoever does and teaches them, he shall be called great in the kingdom of heaven. ..."* (Matthew 5:17,19)

Jesus did not absolve the Law, He fulfilled the penalty of breaking God's Law for us. He also says that whoever does and teaches them, shall be called great in the Kingdom of Heaven. So, continually making choices that break the commandments is not an option if you're pursing freedom.

Jesus also summed up the Law with these two commandments:

> *"Jesus said to him, "'You shall love the Lord your God with all your heart, with all your soul, and with all your mind.' This is the first and great commandment. And the second is like it: 'You shall love your neighbor as yourself.' On these two commandments hang all the Law and the Prophets."* (Matthew 22:36-40)

Love God. Love People. But you can't say you truly love God if you aren't following His commandments. And, you can't say you truly love people, if you aren't encouraging them to live according to God's Truth.

Many people and doctrines may tell you that you can believe in Jesus Christ and be saved, but you can continue to make choices that do not align with the commands nor heart of God. This simply isn't true.

Scripture tells us, "...*and do not be entangled again with a yoke of bondage.*"

When you accept Jesus Christ as your Lord and Savior, you accept the new way of life God DESTINED you to live. This new life, this made free life, is defined by God, not you, me or anyone else. This new life requires a restored heart. It requires a new way of thinking. It requires a new way of acting.

Each of the following chapters will encourage and equip you to walk out the new life you've been given in Jesus Christ.

22) Are you committed to stand in the liberty by which Christ has made you free? _____

23) Are you committed to not be entangled again with a yoke of bondage? _____

Notes:

_____
_____
_____
_____
_____
_____

Session 3

Made Free Workbook

The Holy Spirit, Spirit of Truth

"However, when He, the Spirit of truth, has come, He will guide you into all truth; for He will not speak on His own authority, but whatever He hears He will speak; and He will tell you things to come."
(John 16:13)

The Holy Spirit is your Teacher, Helper, and Comforter. He is the One who will lead you to be made free and help you maintain your freedom in Christ Jesus. He is essential in equipping you to fulfill God's purpose for your life. The Holy Spirit is the One who will bring the peace of God into your life when your heart aches and He comforts you through the seasons of grief life brings.

The Holy Spirit is your life-long companion. His singular purpose is to manifest the Truth of God in your life. He is relentless in His responsibility to reveal the goodness of God in everything. He is uncompromising in bringing forth the Will of God to be accomplished in you, through you and even in spite of you.

I want you to let that seek deep into your spirit. The Holy Spirit is uncompromising in bringing forth the Will of God. This is not about force, but about revelation.

This means, He will not settle for anything less than God's Will for your life. Thus, this is the battle of wills. Yours and God's. Spoiler alert…God's Will is right.

I am currently aware of only three instances the Holy Spirit will relent and let you have your way. The first is to teach you a lesson about demanding your personal will over the hope God has for your life. The second is quenching Him. The third is blaspheming Him, which is denying Him. If you deny the Spirit of God, that means you deny God. Not a wise choice for anyone to make.

Read 1 Samuel 8. Samuel was growing old and his sons did not walk in the ways of the Lord. The people wanted a king, *just like every other nation*. That is important. God told them the consequences of having a king over them. The people kept demanding, so God allowed them to have what they asked for. Low and behold, what came to pass was exactly what God said would happen.

The Holy Spirit will yield to your will, ONLY when God tells Him too. This isn't God giving up. It's teaching you, okay, you think you know best, here you go, learn for yourself. Then, He patiently waits until you either yield, or unfortunately with some, dig your heels in deeper and keep rebelling.

1) Take a moment and ask the Holy Spirit to bring to your remembrance a situation where you ask God for something, and He didn't do it, but you went ahead and did it on you own. Paraphrase it here:
_____
_____
_____
_____

2) What was the outcome?
_____
_____
_____
_____

3) When you realized it wasn't what you had thought or hoped for, what did you do?

_____
_____
_____
_____

4) What did you learn?

_____
_____
_____
_____
_____

5) Do you want to be like everyone else? _____ Now, write down why you do or don't want to be like everyone else?

_____
_____
_____
_____

1 Thessalonians 5:19-20 teaches us,
"Don't suppress the Spirit, and don't stifle those who have a word from the Master. On the other hand, don't be gullible. Check out everything, and keep only what's good. Throw out anything tainted with evil. (THE MESSAGE)

The definition for suppress is, *to overpower and crush: to subdue; to destroy*. You cannot destroy the Holy Spirit, but you can suppress Him enough to cause Him to release you to your own counsel. God, therefore, the Holy Spirit is kind, good and merciful. God, through the Holy Spirit will not impose His Will, but will reveal His Will in order to empower you to make an informed choice. Freewill, greatest gift, greatest challenge.

6) Take a moment and get quiet with the Holy Spirit. Ask Him to reveal any area of your life where you have made the decision to suppress Him. Write it down here:

_____
_____
_____
_____

Ask for forgiveness and ask Him to help you not to quench, to suppress Him in your life again. Do not panic here, asking (prayer), is as simple as this.

"Father, please forgive me for quenching Your Spirit in my life. Holy Spirit help me not to do it again. In Jesus Name, Amen."

Done. Move forward! Don't do it again.

There is a third and it comes with a dire consequence.

> *"Therefore I say to you, every sin and blasphemy will be forgiven men, but the blasphemy against the Spirit will not be forgiven men. Anyone who speaks a word against the Son of Man, it will be forgiven him; but whoever speaks against the Holy Spirit, it will not be forgiven him, either in this age or in the age to come."* (Matthew 12:30-32)

Blasphemy, *an indignity, unmerited, contemptuous conduct, offered to God, by denying that which is due and belong to Him.*

Read Matthew 12:30-32 again.

7) What is Jesus telling you regarding the importance of the Holy Spirit?

_____
_____
_____
_____
_____

8) Ask the Holy Spirit to reveal to you why unmerited, contemptuous conduct towards Him is unforgiveable. Write down what He brings to your mind, don't second guess your thoughts, just write them down. Then, pray about them.

_____
_____
_____
_____

The Holy Spirit is the Spirit of Truth. He is our Helper in revealing God's Truth and learning how to abide in it.

> *"And I will pray the Father, and He will give you another Helper, that He may abide with you forever— the Spirit of truth, whom the world cannot receive, because it neither sees Him nor knows Him; but you know Him, for He dwells with you and will be in you."* (John 14:16-17)

9) Who asks whom to send the Holy Spirit to you? _____

10) Where does the Holy Spirit abide (live)? _____

11) Why can't those who don't know Christ understand the Holy Spirit? _____
_____
_____
_____

This is an important revelation and understanding to have. People who do not accept Christ as their Lord and Savior have great difficulty in conceptualizing the Holy Spirit.

> *"The unspiritual self, just as it is by nature, can't receive the gifts of God's Spirit. There's no capacity for them. They seem like so much silliness. Spirit can be known only by spirit—God's Spirit and our spirits in open communion. Spiritually alive, we have access to everything God's Spirit is doing, and can't be judged by unspiritual critics. Isaiah's question, "Is there anyone around who knows God's Spirit, anyone who knows what he is doing?" has been answered: Christ knows, and we have Christ's Spirit."* (1 Corinthians 2:14-16, THE MESSAGE)

12) *"The unspiritual self, just as it is by nature, can't receive the gifts of God's Spirit."* **What is this saying to you? And, how does it help you to understand the controversy and lack of understanding about the Person of the Holy Spirit?**

_____
_____
_____
_____

13) How can understanding this Truth help you with people's questions, even denial, of the Holy Spirit?

_____
_____
_____
_____

14) Instead of struggling with the Person of the Holy Spirit in ourselves, and with others, Colossians 1:9-11 gives us the key to growing spirit to Spirit:

> *"...do not cease to pray for you, and to ask that you may be filled with the knowledge of His Will in all wisdom and spiritual understanding that you may walk worthy of the Lord, fully pleasing Him, being fruitful in every good work and increasing in the knowledge of God; strengthened with all might, according to His glorious power, for all patience and longsuffering with joy;"*

15) We need to _____ unceasingly so we, and others, are filled with the _____ of His Will in all _____ and _____ understanding. This is so we, and others, are able to walk _____ of the Lord. We can be _____ in every good work and always increasing in the _____ of God. Our _____ will come from God, according to His glorious power.

Let us look at the work of the Holy Spirit. He is so much more than this list, but it's a great starting place to grow in your understanding of Him. For those who already know the Holy Spirit, it's wise to keep studying about Him. It's amazing how new revelations will come as we continue to study the Word.

> *"For as many as are led by the Spirit of God, these are sons of God. For you did not receive the spirit of bondage again to fear, but you received the Spirit of adoption by whom we cry out, "Abba, Father." The Spirit Himself bears witness with our spirit that we are children of God,"* (Romans 8:14-16)

16) Who are those led by the Spirit of God? _____

17) Are we in bondage to fear? _____

18) Who is the spirit of adoption? _____

19) Who adopted us? _____

20) What does Abba, Father mean? _____

21) What does the Spirit bear witness to regarding who you are? _____

The Spirit bears witness you are a child of God, adopted by Him so you can call Him, Daddy God. Daddy, or Papa God, is a term of endearment meant for the closest of bonds. So, during the times you may doubt or feel alone, who will Comfort you and bring Truth to you during those times?

_____

> *"The Spirit of the Lord shall rest upon Him, The Spirit of wisdom and understanding, The Spirit of counsel and might, The Spirit of knowledge and of the fear of the Lord."* (Isaiah 11:2)

22) List the six purposes of the Holy Spirit revealed in Isaiah 11:2:

1) _____; 2) _____; 3) _____;
4) _____; 5) _____; 6) _____.

23) Ask the Holy Spirit to reveal to you the difference of what we call fear and having a fear of the Lord. Then ask Him to give you revelation on fear of the Lord, yet, still calling Him Daddy God.

_____
_____
_____
_____
_____
_____
_____
_____
_____

> *"And the Spirit and the bride say, "Come!" And let him who hears say, "Come!" And let him who thirsts come. Whoever desires, let him take the water of life freely."* (Revelation 22:17)

24) What work is the Holy Spirit doing in Revelation 22:17? _____

25) Who is He crying out to? _____

26) Who is He co-laboring with? _____

Followers of Christ make up the bride of Christ. We co-labor with the Holy Spirit to accomplish the work of the Kingdom of God. This is the greatest purpose anyone can be a part of.

27) Read and write down what each of these verses reveal about the Holy Spirit.

Romans 8:2: _____

Revelation 19:10: _____

Romans 8:15: _____

Romans 1:4: _____

Ephesians 1:17: _____

1 Peter 4:14: _____

The Holy Spirit is also the Spirit of grace (Hebrews 10:29) and the work of hope (Galatians 5:5).

28) Depression is far too prevalent in the world. The antidote to depression is hope. Knowing the Holy Spirit brings the hope of Jesus Christ to us, how does this help us? How does this knowledge help us help others find hope?

_____
_____
_____
_____

The beautiful thing about being able pray for others is it gives us purpose. Purpose and hope drive out loneliness, worthlessness, and hopelessness because we know through the Spirit, our lives make a difference. God is such a genius in how He built into our restoration and freedom the necessity of serving others. The Holy Spirit will lead us to a level of being made free, but continued freedom comes when our lives become about helping others be made free.

The Holy Spirit is the Spirit of the Living God, so He will bring forth the things of God.

He is your Teacher, Counselor and Helper to understand and live out the commands, and blessings, of God. The things of God conflict with our selfish and worldly desires. The Holy Spirit will never condone lying. He will never say it's okay to have sex outside of the covenant of marriage. He will not turn a blind eye to coveting.

> *"Nevertheless I tell you the truth. It is to your advantage that I go away; for if I do not go away, the Helper will not come to you; but if I depart, I will send Him to you. And when He has come, He will convict the world of sin, and of righteousness, and of judgment: of sin, because they do not believe in Me; of righteousness, because I go to My Father and you see Me no more; of judgment, because the ruler of this world is judged.*
>
> *"I still have many things to say to you, but you cannot bear them now. However, when He, the Spirit of truth, has come, He will guide you into all truth; for He will not speak on His own authority, but whatever He hears He will speak; and He will tell you things to come. He will glorify Me, for He will take of what is Mine and declare it to you. All things that the Father has are Mine. Therefore I said that He will take of Mine and declare it to you."* (John 16:7-15)

He convicts me, you, and the world, of sin. The response of a follower of Christ to conviction should be repentance, receiving forgiveness, then moving forward with Christ. The response of a non-follower of Christ to conviction should be repentance, which is God's heart. But the response is too often, anger, bitterness, hatred, and an alignment of like-minded 'sinners' to justify their behavior. This only increases the strength of the bondage.

This is why so many fight against Him and even deny Him. Who likes to be convicted of sin? But when we recognize that sin always leads to destruction, and the Holy Spirit is trying to keep us from being destroyed, conviction becomes easier to work through.

Cooperating with the Holy Spirit is so much easier than fighting against Him. When you cooperate with Him, the fruit is love, joy, peace, longsuffering, kindness, goodness, faithfulness, gentleness, and self-control.

29) Ask the Holy Spirit to reveal any sin you may have knowingly or unknowing committed against God. Write down what comes to your mind immediately, don't argue with it in your mind.

_____
_____
_____
_____

Ask for forgiveness, repent and move forward in Christ.

30) Read Jeremiah 31:34. What does this verse say to you?

_____
_____
_____
_____

31) How does the Truth change how you think about the sin and the power of God's forgiveness?

_____
_____
_____
_____

32) Read John 16:7-15. On whose authority does the Holy Spirit speak? _____

_____

33) Why is this important to know and always remember? _____

_____
_____
_____

34) Who will the Holy Spirit always glorify? _____
_____
_____

35) How does this help you learn to discern the voice of the Holy Spirt?

_____
_____
_____
_____

The Holy Spirit is a gift from God, therefore, to receive Him, you ask the Father to send Him to you. And, you believe you have received Him.

"If you then, being evil, know how to give good gifts to your children, how much more will your heavenly Father give the Holy Spirit to those who ask Him!" (Luke 11:13)

The Holy Spirit is essential in your life. He, through Jesus Christ, is the key to unlock and receive all God has for you.

One very powerful role the Holy Spirit has in the lives of Christ followers is to tell us of things to come. This pertains to our individual lives and the purposes of God, in so much He can entrust us with being told.

Have you ever had a thought that something was going to happen?

Have there been times when you knew you might lose a job, or an accident was about to happen?

The Holy Spirit tells us of things to come so we can be prepared for them. So, when we don't cultivate our relationship with Him, things continually catch us off guard. Our lives are then lived in a rushed, chaotic state of panic. When the Holy Spirit lets us know of things to come, we are prepared, and we respond in peace and wisdom.

Followers of Jesus Christ are to be led by the Holy Spirit.

36) How well is the Holy Spirit operating in your life as your Helper? Write down why and how you can co-operate with Him more.

_____
_____
_____
_____
_____
_____
_____

37) How well is the Holy Spirit operating in your life as your Teacher? Write down why and what changes you need to make for Him to be more active in your life as your Teacher.

_____
_____
_____
_____
_____
_____
_____

38) How well is the Holy Spirit operating in your life as Comforter? Don't limit comfort to times of grief. There are many other situations where we need comfort. Ask Him to reveal those to you and broaden your understanding of being comforted by the Holy Spirit.

_____
_____
_____
_____
_____
_____
_____

39) Ask the Holy Spirit if you can be trusted to be told of the deep things of God. Ask Him what you need to do in order to be able to be entrusted with the riches, the mysteries, of the Kingdom of God.

_____
_____
_____
_____
_____
_____
_____

"Holy Spirit, I ask for You to fill me. I ask that You be my Helper, Teacher and Comforter. I pray You will convict, equip and guide me unto all Truth so that I will be made free for my good and God's glory. In Jesus Name, Amen."

Reality Check

Made Free Workbook

Your New Life Requires Work

"But we all, with unveiled face, beholding as in a mirror the glory of the Lord, are being transformed into the same image from glory to glory, just as by the Spirit of the Lord." (2 Corinthians 3:18)

Transformation is what being Made Free is all about. It's about transformation *towards an intended* result. God's intended result, not yours. And, sorry, there is not an easy button to push to transform your life from its current state to glory to glory to glory. Yes, the process never stops while we are on this earth. Real change, a real-life change, requires commitment and perseverance to see the promises come to fruition.

> *"Whenever, though, they turn to face God as Moses did, God removes the veil and there they are—face-to-face! They suddenly recognize that God is a living, personal presence, not a piece of chiseled stone. And when God is personally present, a living Spirit, that old, constricting legislation is recognized as obsolete. We're free of it! All of us! Nothing between us and God, our faces shining with the brightness of his face. And so we are transfigured much like the Messiah, our lives gradually becoming brighter and more beautiful as God enters our lives and **we become like him**."* (1 Corinthians 3:16-18, THE MESSAGE, emphasis added)

A decision to accept Jesus Christ as our Lord and Savior sets us on a new path of life. It sets us on a path to live connected to our Creator and following His commands. These commands are not to control us, but to set us free. Freedom as defined by God's standard, not the world's claim that it's freedom to do whatever we when, whenever we want, and with whomever we want. The world's definition of freedom will not set you free, it will devour and destroy you. Time will always prove this as true.

"...they turn to face God" When we accept Jesus Christ as Lord, we turn from our old ways, the separation from God has been removed, and we stand before God, face to face. Not just after a physical death, but now, while we are living on earth. You now live your life face to face with God.

God is a living being. He is a personal presence. His Spirit is alive and well. There is nothing between God and us. Our face, our countenance, should begin to shine as we spend more and more time with Him. Our minds are renewed in His presence.

This is not a 3-day fast, a 21-day cleanse, or even a 90-day makeover. This is a new way of living to gradually become brighter and more beautiful as God enters our lives and we are Made Free.

It's also not about cookie cutter Christianity. Yes, there are non-negotiables on how all followers of Christ should live. But it has nothing to do with hair style, clothes you wear, boisterous or subdued personalities, economic standing or position.

It has everything to do with cultivating a life to live face to face with God and having the heart and mind of Christ. God is relentless in this transformation process because it breaks His heart to see His creations not living as He created us to live.

Think about what it means to *"turn to face God"*.

1) How does this change your perspective about cultivating a relationship with God? _____
_____
_____
_____

2) How does knowing God can look directly into your eyes and you can look into His affect how you view:

God: _____
_____
_____
_____

Yourself: _____
_____
_____
_____

He provides everything necessary to accomplish being transformed from glory to glory. The rest requires work on our part.

Read the definitions of work.

> Work, *to operate; to produce effects by action or influence.*
>
> Work, *to obtain by diligence.*
>
> Work, *to bring into any state by action.*

3) What does this mean to you in your Made Free journey?
_____
_____
_____
_____

Many people allow confusion regarding "work" to earn from God and "work" needed to obtain by diligence being transformed and set free. "Work" to earn anything from God, such as His love, grace, mercy, is legalism, and impossible. You cannot "work" to earn salvation or righteousness.

"Work" motivated to become like Christ is understanding grace and is fueled by a passion to keep falling in love with Almighty God.

4) Do you find yourself trying to 'earn' God's love, His forgiveness, His favor? _____

If yes, why? Ask the Holy Spirit to help you answer this. _____

_____
_____
_____
_____

Consistent diligence is required to pursue the promises of God. Perseverance to hold fast to His promises especially through the challenges life brings will transform your character. As your character becomes more and more Christlike, the hope in Christ flourishes in your life. This hope will never disappoint you because it is rooted in the love of God and confirmed in our hearts by the Holy Spirit.

You become made free by God's Word by continual adherence to them through diligence regardless of the circumstances you find yourself in.

5) What challenges do you already know you'll encounter as you 'work' to change your current lifestyle to one God has promised you can have?

_____
_____
_____
_____

6) What ways of thinking are you going to have to 'work' at, so they no longer hold you hostage to destructive behavior?

_____
_____
_____
_____

7) What behaviors are you going to have to 'work' at to change, so they do not set you up for unnecessary challenges and discouraging attitudes?

_____
_____
_____
_____

God's Truth will confront every aspect of your life. At that moment of confrontation, you have a choice, trust God, or continue in paths less than the goodness of God.

    Confront, *to stand face to face in full view; to stand in front.*

    Confront, *to stand in direct opposition, to oppose.*

8) What thoughts, beliefs, behaviors, has God's Truth confronted thus far in your made free process?

_____
_____
_____
_____

Ask the Holy Spirit to guide you through the answers of the following questions. You may think you believe one way, but the Holy Spirit may reveal something different.

9) Do you believe God's Truth is absolute? Yes / No

Why or why not?

_____
_____
_____
_____

10) If yes, how do your thoughts/attitude towards the below align with His Truths?

Him:

_____
_____
_____
_____

Yourself:

_____
_____
_____
_____

Others:

_____
_____

11) If no, what are some of the differences? For example, you may believe God is distance, or doesn't involve Himself in the details of every day life.

Him:

Yourself:

Others:

12) How does your behavior align with the degree to which you believe God's Truth is absolute?

13) How much of your life, your thoughts, decision making process, actions, etc. is influenced by man's, the world's, opinions?

Don't push past the above question too quickly. Pray it through with the Holy Spirit. We are all influenced to varying degrees by the environments we are exposed to. God, through His Word and Spirit, will confront everything not in alignment with His Truth. Sometimes He does it all at once, most times, it's a gradual process, layer by layer. I believe He does this because of His abounding love for us and He knows we can only take so much transformation at a time.

This is also where many people allow confusion or doubt to enter in. Let's say God has said you need to forgive so and so. You, through gritted teeth, start the process to forgive them. It starts with saying it and your heart starts to soften. Then, one day, you realize you're no longer carrying bitterness or anger towards that person.

Throughout that process, you hear the manipulative and destructive voice of the enemy saying things like, they don't deserve your forgiveness; you don't really need to forgive them. But you trust it's in your and their best interests to trust in God's Truth: forgiveness sets you free.

Time passes and you have a thought that you haven't really forgiven them. Two things may be occurring here. One is the enemy is trying to get you to doubt. Ignore him and pray to the Lord. The second is the Lord taking you to a higher level of healing and restoration, which usually comes with a new revelation and understanding about the situation. Your response isn't necessarily about forgiveness. Your response is, "Lord, what is it you're trying to reveal to me?" Then, proceed accordingly.

He may reveal you haven't fully forgiven them yet. It's simply the next level of being made free. It may be the Lord trying to show you a different perspective so you can use your experience to encourage someone else.

We are called to live differently than the ways of man and we are not to live bound to the things of the world. We are to live with the unshakable and eternal Truth of God as our foundation. He will teach us His ways and we are to live our lives in the freedom of His paths.

We are in a marathon, not a sprint. We train (work) for the long journey, the glorious prize found in the fullness of Jesus Christ. As our heart and mind is transformed, the work we've done produces the blessings of God in our lives.

Yes, prosperity can be one of those blessings. Favor. Protection. Miracles. All of those are products, evidence, of the blessings of the Truth of God's way of life at work in our lives. Do not lessen the value of fruit produced in our nature of self-control, gentleness, faithfulness, goodness, kindness, patience, peace, joy and love.

The worth of the fruit of our labor in our lives is more valuable than gold and precious jewels. They are more important than a large bank account and big house. Having peace in the midst of a great challenge is priceless and worth every ounce of 'work' the Holy Spirit requires of us to be made free by God's Truth.

Are you having trouble believing me?

- Have you ever faced being laid-off at work? What would you give to be able to be at peace with whatever the outcome?
- Have you experienced abuse? What would you give to be shown kindness?
- Has someone lashed out in anger at you? What would you give to be able to show self-control and be able to respond and bring healing to the pain that drives the anger?
- Have you lost someone you loved? What would you give to know there is joy in the midst of grief?
- Have you experienced worthlessness? What would you give to know love?
- Is there someone you love in bondage to depression? What would you give to show them hope?

There are far greater rewards in the Kingdom of God than material things. It requires work to produce the results.

14) What work are you willing to do in order to be transformed into who God desires you to be?

_____
_____
_____
_____

15) What price are you willing to pay in order to live FREE?

_____
_____
_____
_____
_____
_____
_____
_____
_____
_____
_____
_____
_____
_____
_____
_____
_____
_____
_____
_____

Work towards the goal for the prize of the upward call of God in Christ Jesus!

Session 4

Made Free Workbook

New Creation in Christ

"Therefore, if anyone is in Christ, he is a new creation; old things have passed away; behold, all things have become new." (2 Corinthians 5:17)

We are born with a nature that is bent towards committing sin. Remember, sin is conducting oneself in any manner below God's standard of holiness. It is an impossible standard…outside of a life lived in Christ Jesus. We need to be taught right from wrong, and that standard of right and wrong must be defined by God's standard. Otherwise, it is shifting sand as the ideals and culture of man change constantly.

Our nature leans towards self-preservation and has an inward focus. Toddlers do not have to be taught how to lie. The ability to lie comes to them all on their own. They could have chocolate all over their face, partial cookie in one hand, and they will deny they took that cookie when asked.

Think about a time when you were confronted about something you may have done wrong. Be honest with yourself here, your first instinct was most likely in the form of self-preservation, which means denying, justifying, or even angry accusation to turn it back on the one doing the confronting.

Our nature becomes more bent towards committing sin when one experiences hurt, abandonment, disappointments, abuse, manipulation and lies. Our environment and exposure to these and other experiences contrary to the Truth of God and His goodness reinforce our old nature of self-preservation…and it can manifest in harmful choices creating life cycles that lead to destruction.

Our nature, our pre-Christ old nature, with its unhealthy, self-defeating mindset and thought patterns has been replaced with a new nature in Christ Jesus. You have been given the opportunity, through Jesus Christ and God's Truths, to be made free. You are a new creation, and you have been given a new nature.

Your new nature in Christ will bend you towards pursuing living with the heart and mind of Christ. This means if there is anything out of alignment in your life, it will be addressed by the Holy Spirit. Your new nature will continually confront, and will eventually overcome, the old nature in every area of your life. You will develop a healthy, balanced, and Scripturally-sound view of God, yourself and others.

Let's go back to the example of being confronted about something we've done wrong.

Our old nature response is some form of self-preservation.

Our new nature, new creation response usually depends upon the degree of healing and security we have developed in our identity in Christ and the depths of our relationship with God.

Those who are recent to being made into a new creation do their best to respond with less self-preservation. But what will happen if you don't deal with it through a godly response, the Holy Spirit will make you uncomfortable. This occurs because old and new are at war with each other, they cannot coexist. It's the Holy Spirit's job to help you get all aspects of the old way of life out of you. He is very good at His job. He will continue to bug (convict), you until you either yield, or tell Him to be quiet. He will relent at your request. But know this, by relenting, He is not quitting His job. He is simply allowing you to endure the fullness of the consequences necessary for you to learn the lesson God wants you to learn.

Those who have been a new creation for a bit of time and have been pursing living the commands of God hopefully will respond by taking responsibility for their actions. They will apologize, ask what needs to be done to make it right, ask for forgiveness and move on. They are learning to lean on God and trust He will see them through whatever happens. The know they are a new creation. They know they are His and He will work things out to their good.

Those who have been a new creation for a while shouldn't have done whatever it was in the first place. The commands of God set boundaries for us. There are some things we should know not to do because they are quite clear in the Word of God. If not, then the Holy Spirit would have warned you not to do it, and a conscious decision was made not to heed His voice.

If the decision was made not to heed His voice, then usually the Holy Spirit will tell us to make it right immediately. If we chose not to, the peace of God that has been cultivated through our relationship with Him will lessen. It is a very empty feeling when God's peace is removed because we've chosen disobedience.

The good news is His peace returns when we repent, are forgiven, and keep pursing Him. He is a gracious, merciful God. Fair warning here, do not take the grace and mercy of God for granted. The Bible is very clear about consequences for those who, even though they profess to know Christ, continually choose to be disobedient.

You are a new creation! Begin to live like one.

> "Therefore if anyone is in Christ [that is, grafted in, joined to Him by faith in Him as Savior], he is a new creature [reborn and renewed by the Holy Spirit]; the old things [the previous moral and spiritual condition] have passed away. Behold, new things have come [because spiritual awakening brings a new life]."
> (2 Corinthians 5:17, AMP)

1) How does it make you feel knowing you have been reborn and renewed by the Holy Spirit in Christ Jesus?

_____
_____
_____
_____

2) How does knowing you no longer have to live according to the old things, the previous moral and spiritual condition you have been in?

3) How does it make you feel knowing that all things in your life can become new because you have been awoken spiritually to new life?

4) How does this Truth help you deal with things you may have been told or you have thought about yourself? Examples: "I couldn't help it." "You'll never change." "I'll never be able to live like Christ."

5) What are some thoughts, behaviors, or responses to things you do, but don't really like doing them? Ask the Holy Spirit to help you. Be intentional about engaging with Him in your journey. He is your Helper, Comforter and Teacher.

6) How does it make you feel knowing those things you don't like about yourself no longer define you, and better yet, can be replaced with the promises of being a new creation?

7) How much importance do you give to man's opinion towards/about you?

8) Do you give more credibility towards God's or man's thoughts toward and about you? Why?

_____
_____
_____
_____

9) How much do you allow emotions to dictate how you think about:

God: _____
_____
_____
_____

Yourself: _____
_____
_____
_____

Family: _____
_____
_____
_____

People: _____
_____
_____
_____

The world around you: _____
_____
_____
_____

10) How much do you think your emotions or other people's opinion influence how you feel/think about what God has to say on the same subjects above?

_____
_____
_____
_____

As a new creation in Christ, old thoughts, old principles, and old practices are going to be confronted if they are not in alignment with God's Truth. Your decision to follow Christ aligned you with God and His standard of living. He, through the power of the Holy Spirit, will continually transform your heart, mind, and body, thereby transforming your nature to be as Christ's.

Yes, you have been immediately made into a new creation through your faith in Jesus Christ. Old things no longer hold you in bondage nor define who you are and what you are capable of. But just like toddlers, we have to be taught God's way.

You have been given a new heart.

> *"I will give you a new heart and put a new spirit within you; I will take the heart of stone out of your flesh and give you a heart of flesh."* (Ezekiel 36:26)

I remember when I was trying to get my life in alignment with God. I never doubted Jesus Christ as Lord and Savior, but there were numerous times when I didn't live my life with Him as my Savior. Those times bruised, battered and hardened my heart. There was a time when I bound all my emotions into a very tight little box. My mindset was to just get through life and then squeak into the back door of heaven. Life was simply too painful to feel.

That is not what God desires for His children. So, His Spirit led me to a ladies' discipleship class. I knew I should take it. But my biggest fear was knowing He was going to make me feel again. I knew He was going to soften my heart, ask me to unpack all the disappointments, guilt, shame, unworthiness and let Him heal and restore me. He was going to get me back on track to be the new creation I was meant to be.

11) How does it make you feel knowing you have been given a new heart?

_____
_____
_____
_____

Because of my life choices and events, the first thing God dealt during this season of my restoration was being able to accept His forgiveness. There was a part of me that knew He loved me. But I simply couldn't move forward in developing a deeper relationship with Him and living as a new creation because I just couldn't comprehend a holy, life-giving God forgiving abortion.

I went to class and when the leaders prayed for me, the Lord gave me a vision. I was kneeling at the Cross of Jesus Christ, hand on the Cross, head bowed with my body trembling in tears. The Blood of Jesus Christ then covered me from head to toe. It was through that gift, my heart softened, and I have never doubted the forgiving power of Jesus Christ. And, no one has ever been able to shake that Truth in my life. I have been forgiven. Yes, there are still consequences. I still experience grief. My heart aches every time someone mentions abortion. But abortion does not define me, and it does not separate me from the love of God found in Christ Jesus. I have been forgiven; I am a new creation.

12) What are you holding in your heart that you know separates you from experiencing more of God's love and promises?

_____

13) Ask the Holy Spirit to reveal to you any hardness you are holding in your heart. Write them down.

14) Ask the Holy Spirit to help you find verses in the Bible that speak healing and restoration to those areas. Write them down. Biblegateway.com is a great resource. Do a search of key words like healing, restoration, restore, etc. Then scroll through the verses until one makes you pause. That, most likely, is the verse you need to bring healing.

15) Take a few moments and put on some quiet worship music. Spend some time in the presence of God, talking to Him about the areas of hardness in your heart. Write down what He reveals to you.

We are not meant to have hardened hearts. God wants our hearts to be as His heart; a heart able to love and be loved.

You have been given a new mind.

You can no longer think how you used to think. You are a new creation. You, through God's Word and the leading of the Holy Spirit, can learn to think like Christ. Impossible, I think not because God's Word tells me we can. If we so choose to.

> *"For "who has known the mind of the Lord that he may instruct Him?" But **we have the mind of Christ.**"* (1 Corinthians 2:16, emphasis added)

We learn to have the mind of Christ by putting boundaries on everything that has to do with our minds.

> *"that you put off, concerning your former conduct, the old man which grows corrupt according to the deceitful lusts, and **be renewed in the spirit of your mind,** and that you put on the new man which was created according to God, in true righteousness and holiness."* (Ephesians 4:22-24, emphasis added)

As a new creation, we can no longer engage in former conduct if it was outside of the righteousness and holiness God has called us to live in. The mind is where we process information and make decisions on how to respond. Our minds are renewed by the Word and presence of God. The more of His Truths we have in our mind, therefore heart, the easier it is to base our thoughts, behaviors and responses in alignment with His Will. This creates an atmosphere in and around us conducive to abiding in the blessings of God.

> *"And do not be conformed to this world, but be transformed by the renewing of your mind, that you may prove what is that good and acceptable and perfect will of God."* (Romans 12:2)

16) Romans 12:2 tells us to, *"do not be conformed to this world."* **What does this mean to you?**

_____
_____
_____
_____

17) How is your mind transformed?

_____
_____
_____
_____

18) What is the purpose of having a transformed mind?

_____
_____
_____
_____

19) Imagine what it would be like proving the good and acceptable and perfect will of God. What do you think your life would look like?

_____
_____
_____
_____

> *"casting down arguments and every high thing that exalts itself against the knowledge of God, bringing every thought into captivity to the obedience of Christ,"* (2 Corinthians 10:5)

20) What are key disciplines in 2 Corinthians 10:5 to having your mind transformed?

i) _____ down _____

ii) _____ high thing that _____ itself against the _____ of God

iii) bringing _____ thought into _____

21) Why do you think it's so important to bring EVERY argument, high thing, and thought into captivity, *"…to the obedience of Christ,"*?

_____
_____
_____
_____

22) What are some thoughts you think about yourself that have not been brought under Christ?

_____
_____
_____
_____

Your body no longer belongs to you.

> *"So here's what I want you to do, God helping you: Take your everyday, ordinary life—your sleeping, eating, going-to-work, and walking-around life—and place it before God as an offering. Embracing what God does for you is the best thing you can do for him. Don't become so well-adjusted to your culture that you fit into it without even thinking. Instead, fix your attention on God. You'll be changed from the inside out. Readily recognize what he wants from you, and quickly respond to it. Unlike the culture around you, always dragging you down to its level of immaturity, God brings the best out of you, develops well-formed maturity in you."* (Romans 12:1-2, THE MESSAGE)

As a new creation, every aspect of our life is an offering to God. The routine things we do every day is an opportunity for God to bring out the best in us. We are changed from the inside out by God. This includes how we treat our bodies. The human body is a miraculous work of genius by God.

Some interesting facts about the body:

- The human brain has a memory capacity equivalent to more than four terabytes on a hard drive…for non-tech people, this is an overwhelming amount of knowledge. Philippians 4:8, *"Finally, brethren, whatever things are true, whatever things are noble, whatever things are just, whatever things are pure, whatever things are lovely, whatever things are of good report, if there is any virtue and if there is anything praiseworthy—meditate on these things."*

- 50,000 cells died and were replaced by new ones in the amount of time it took to read this sentence. Isaiah 44:24, *"Thus says the Lord, your Redeemer, **And He who formed you from the womb:** "I am the Lord, who makes all things, Who stretches out the heavens all alone, Who spreads abroad the earth by Myself;"* (emphasis added)

- Teeth are the only part of the body that cannot heal themselves. Every other part of our bodies has the capability to heal.

- The strongest muscle in the human body is the tongue. Proverbs 18:21, *"Death and life are in the power of the tongue, and those who love it will eat its fruit."*

- A person would die quicker from a total lack of sleep then from hunger. Exodus 20:8-11, *"Remember the Sabbath day, to keep it holy. Six days you shall labor and do all your work,* **but the seventh day is the Sabbath of the Lord your God.** *In it you shall do no work: you, nor your son, nor your daughter, nor your male servant, nor your female servant, nor your cattle, nor your stranger who is within your gates. For in six days the Lord made the heavens and the earth, the sea, and all that is in them,* **and rested the seventh day.** *Therefore the Lord blessed the Sabbath day and hallowed it."* (emphasis added)

You were created by God. Your body was fearfully and wonderfully made. Your body is designed to glorify God, not to be mistreated or become an idol.

We were created mind, body, spirit. When one of those areas is not cared for, all of them are affected. This causes us to function out of balance.

23) What care do you currently give your body?

_____
_____
_____
_____

24) What areas of your life where you are mistreating your body?

_____
_____
_____
_____

25) What changes can you start making to take better care of your body?

_____
_____
_____
_____

26) How much of your time do you spend more time staring at, analyzing or comparing your body to others?
1 Timothy 4:8 tells us, *"For bodily exercise profits a little, but godliness is profitable for all things..."* This is referring to priorities and balance in our lives.

_____
_____
_____
_____

1 Corinthians 6:19-20 teaches us, *"Or do you not know that your body is the temple of the Holy Spirit who is in you, whom you have from God, and you are not your own? For you were bought at a price; therefore glorify God in your body and in your spirit, which are God's."*

27) Knowing the body is the temple of the Holy Spirit, how does this change how you evaluate and treat your body?

_____
_____
_____
_____

New Creation, New Spirit.

Ezekiel 36:26-27, *" I will give you a new heart and put a new spirit within you; I will take the heart of stone out of your flesh and give you a heart of flesh. I will put My Spirit within you and cause you to walk in My statutes, and you will keep My judgments and do them."* God is speaking to the house of Israel in these verses. They are just as true and relevant to those who confess Jesus Christ as Lord today.

As a new creation in Christ, we are given a new Spirit. He is the Spirit of the Living God. He is given to us for the purpose of teaching, guiding and helping us to walk in God's ways.

The new Spirit within us will never contradict the commands of God. So, every time we think or behave outside of God's ways, the Spirit will convict us. This isn't to manipulate and control us, it is to protect us and enable us to live productive and purposeful lives.

We must commit our lives to living by the Spirit of God. Otherwise, we are constantly living beneath our God-desired potential and we will be at war within ourselves. Galatians 6:7-9 puts it this way, *"Do not be deceived, God is not mocked; for whatever a man sows, that he will also reap. For he who sows to his flesh will of the flesh reap corruption, but he who sows to the Spirit will of the Spirit reap everlasting life. And let us not grow weary while doing good, for in due season we shall reap if we do not lose heart. Therefore, as we have opportunity, let us do good to all, especially to those who are of the household of faith."*

You can't fool God. Whatever you "feed", either your own desires or the Spirit within you, you will reap. Sowing to the flesh, lying, stealing, overeating, under eating, shopping too much, drinking too much, all of these feeds the flesh, and the desire for them increases. Then, you become a slave to them, you are in bondage to them. This also includes what you expose yourself to. If you expose yourself to pornography, violence, explicit words, hateful words and actions, they too, feed your flesh. And, the desire for them will grow. The desire for them will war against the Spirit until you make the decision which one you will yield to.

Jesus says in John 8:34, *"whoever commits a sin is a slave of sin."* Reminder, sin is anything in disobedience to God's commands. Sin harms us, and if left unchecked, will destroy us.

28) Take a brutally honest look at your life. Ask the Holy Spirit to show you what are you feeding. List everything that comes to your mind.

_____
_____
_____
_____

29) How does this list make you feel?

_____
_____
_____
_____

30) What changes in your life do you need to make to stop sowing to the flesh?

_____
_____
_____
_____

> *"...but he who sows to the Spirit will of the Spirit reap everlasting life.*

31) What areas of your life does the Holy Spirit tell you to start sowing to?

_____
_____
_____
_____

You have a new nature.

We are partakers of the divine nature of Jesus Christ. Our new nature will compel us to pursue a life worthy of the goodness of God. Our new nature no longer hungers after the things of the world, but hungers after relationship with God, with a heart set on pleasing Him and doing the things He calls us to do.

We still have to work to put our old nature out of operation. You have to change old habits and replace them with God-focused, Christ-like ones. It will be a lifelong process, but the battle becomes easier because the more you get to know God, the less you want to do anything that isn't according to His goodness.

32) What does it mean to you to know you have been given a divine nature?

_____
_____
_____
_____

33) Your new nature can overcome damaging habits, unhealthy cycles in your life. What does that mean to you?

_____
_____
_____
_____

34) How does it change your mindset knowing you live by God's rules, and not your own?

_____
_____
_____
_____

35) James 4:17 says, *"Therefore, to him who knows to do good and does not do it, to him it is sin."* What does this verse reveal to you?

About your life lived in the Lord:

_____
_____
_____
_____
_____
_____
_____
_____

Regarding others' personal walk with the Lord:

_____
_____
_____
_____
_____
_____
_____
_____

Your old self has passed away. Start living as a new creature!

Session 5

Made Free Workbook

Kingdom Mindset

"If then you were raised with Christ, seek those things which are above, where Christ is, sitting at the right hand of God. Set your mind on things above, not on things on the earth. For you died, and your life is hidden with Christ in God. When Christ who is our life appears, then you also will appear with Him in glory."
(Colossians 3:1-4)

Our personal agenda, desires, and will is supposed to die when we accepted Jesus Christ as our Lord and Savior. They are destined to be replaced with the agenda, desires and Will of God for us and His Kingdom purposes…if we stay the course.

There is a higher purpose at work and its intended to be accomplished while we are here on earth. Otherwise, God would take each of us home the moment we accepted Jesus Christ as Savior. He wants us to inherit a portion of His Kingdom while we are still on earth. The fullness will come with the return of Jesus Christ.

It's important to learn how to live in the 'now' with the Kingdom-mindset of God's Kingdom come, His Will be done on earth as it is in heaven. And, yes, it is possible, because if it wasn't, Jesus wouldn't have told us to pray in such a manner.

A Kingdom-mindset seeks and sets itself on the things above. Everything is approached with the question, "God, what is Your Will in this situation?" A Kingdom-mindset accepts nothing less than God's Will to be done in any circumstance. The lion share of knowing God's Will is found in the Word of God. So you need to be a student of the Word. The remaining portion is discovered through relationship. He reveals His purposes to those He prepares to receive them and trusts they will be carried out according to His desire.

A Kingdom-mindset does not neglect the necessities nor realities of this world. But a mind set on things above recognizes that the realities of this world must yield to the authority and Will of the Kingdom of God. Sometimes it's challenging to see because of the fallen world we live in, and the complexities of God's gift of freewill. The more Kingdom-minded you become, the more evident it will become that He works all things to our good and His glory…and yes, all things.

There is also nothing wrong with prosperity. God provides and God blesses. However, prosperity should never become your identity, value, nor an idol in your life. A Kingdom-mindset has no issue with prosperity for themselves or others because they recognize all of it belongs to God. We are simply the stewards.

1) What does it mean to you to *"seek the things that are above"*?

_____
_____

2) What does it mean to you to *"set your mind on things that are above"*?

3) What areas of your life do you have a less than Kingdom-mindset about? (Examples: This is the way it has always been; things will never get better; I guess it's just meant to be.)

The prayer Jesus taught the disciples to pray gives us insight into developing a Kingdom-mindset. Please keep in mind, the Words Jesus gave us should not become vain repetition. It's meant to teach us how to approach the Father and ask for His provision, heart and guidance.

"Our Father in heaven, hallowed be Your name."

4) How does this opening sentence in the prayer Jesus gave us position the Father?

"Your Kingdom come, your Will be done on earth as it is in heaven?"

5) Whose Kingdom is this prayer asking to come forth? Who is being asked to bring it forth?

6) Whose Will are you asking to be done on earth? Why is this important to keep in mind?

God is all-knowing and all-powerful. He doesn't, but He is more than able to force His Will on us. He can wipe humanity out with a Word. Instead, He chose and created a path for redemption and restoration.

7) Why do you think Jesus Christ asks us to pray for God's Kingdom to be done here on earth as it is in heaven?

_____
_____
_____
_____

8) Do you believe it's possible for God's Will to be done on earth as it is in heaven? Why or Why not?

_____
_____
_____
_____

Every person who calls Jesus Christ Lord has a global purpose to fulfill the Great Commission. Jesus' last command to every follower of Christ is to, *"Go therefore and make disciples of all the nations, baptizing them in the name of the Father and of the Son and of the Holy Spirit, teaching them to observe all things that I have commanded you; and lo, I am with you always, even to the end of the age."* (Matthew 28:19-20)

No one is exempt from this command and each of us will be held to account by God in our role to fulfill Jesus' command. It's not only your Pastor's responsibility. It's not just for those who have written a book, have more followers on Twitter or friends on Facebook, or have a larger platform of influence. It's not just those who are on staff at a church. It is the responsibility of every single one of us, regardless of our title, the size of our bank account, or our pasts. There will be no excuse to justify our lack in fulfilling the commission of Jesus Christ.

You may be called to share the gospel to one. You may be called to millions. But you are called to fulfill the commission of Christ. A Kingdom-mindset seeks out what God has destined for them in the global commission. They learn not to be overly concerned with what others are accomplishing, because they recognize it's for the Kingdom. It's important to know what is going on in the global Body of Christ, but it should NEVER become a distraction, source of coveting, or an excuse to your personal calling in fulfilling the Great Commission.

9) How much of your time do you spend chasing after other followers of Christ rather than seeking God's plan for you?

_____
_____
_____
_____

10) How can you start fulfilling the global commission of Christ?

_____
_____
_____
_____

A Kingdom-mindset sets their mind on taking up their personal position.

11) Do you know what your personal position is? Why or Why not?

_____

12) What are you doing to excel in your personal position and glorify God?

1 Corinthians 12 instructs us on how God gifts and positions the Body to accomplish His plans and purposes in and through us. Cultivating a Kingdom-mindset embraces God's plan and trusts God to know what is best for us and for others. This mindset helps us deal with insecurities, jealousies and fears. The Holy Spirit leads us to tell ourselves, and others, "if God gifts and positions me here, then I'm good enough, worthy and able to fulfill this position."

Read 1 Corinthians 12.

13) How does 1 Corinthians 12 address who is really in charge of gifts and positions?

14) How does this truth deal with the excuse, "if I were so and so, or had such and such, then I would be able to accomplish _____?"

15) What do you need to do to set your mind on the higher perspective on gifts and positions?

16) Are you too focused on the future, rather than being Kingdom-minded about where God has you right now? What can you do to embrace what you have right now with excellence?

A Kingdom-mindset trusts God in how He gifts and positions His people. God values and honors every position.

17) How does this truth help you cultivate a Kingdom-mindset?

_____
_____
_____
_____

A Kingdom-mindset is necessary inside and outside of church walls. It's not just for Sundays, but for every day of the week. It doesn't change when our location changes.

> Acts 10:38 tells us, *"how God anointed Jesus of Nazareth with the Holy Spirit and with power, who went about doing good and healing all who were oppressed by the devil, for God was with Him."*

18) If we're supposed to have the same mindset as Jesus, what does this verse tell us about what we should be doing?

_____
_____
_____
_____

19) Who defines what is good? _____

20) How does this shape our behavior and our interaction with others?

_____
_____
_____
_____

If it's God who defines what is good, then a Kingdom-mindset thinks, speaks and behaves by His standard of good. A Kingdom-mindset doesn't lower itself to the world's definition of good. And, a Kingdom-mindset doesn't change God's definitions of good when personal opinions or cultural trends try to insert themselves.

You, as Christ was, are anointed with the Holy Spirit and with power to go about doing good and healing all those who are oppressed by the devil. For God is with you and He is for you.

21) How does this truth change your perspective about yourself?

_____
_____
_____
_____

22) How does this truth change your perspective on how you view the world?

_____
_____
_____
_____

Proclaim this over your life, *"The Spirit of the Lord is upon me. I am anointed to preach the gospel to the poor. I am sent to heal the brokenhearted with the love of God. I am equipped to proclaim the liberty of Christ to the captives. I am anointed to recover the sight of those who are blind. My life is a testimony that who the Son sets free is free indeed."*

Doing good is loving God and loving people. Kingdom-minded is loving people with the love of God and the Truth of His Word—even when it is challenging, inconvenient and may hurt our own heart (to a degree). Doing good never encourages a victim-mentality, nor does it enable a person to remain in a place of bondage. Doing good always loves people to a place of restoration, first to God, then within themselves and then to others.

Remember, a Kingdom-mindset recognizes that all followers of Christ are not gifted nor positioned the same. So, my "doing good" may not look like your "doing good". But we are working towards the same goal, *"Your Kingdom come, Your Will be done on earth as it is in heaven."* Together, we can accomplish so much more than individually.

23) What are some of your thoughts in cultivating a Kingdom-mindset?

_____
_____
_____
_____
_____
_____
_____
_____

Read Joshua 5.

Verses 13-15, NIV, gives interesting insight into a Kingdom-mindset.

> *"Now when Joshua was near Jericho, he looked up and saw a man standing in front of him with a drawn sword in his hand. Joshua went up to him and asked, "Are you for us or for our enemies?" "Neither," he replied, "but as commander of the army of the Lord I have now come." Then Joshua fell facedown to the ground in reverence, and asked him, "What message does my Lord have for his servant?" The commander of the Lord's army replied, "Take off your sandals, for the place where you are standing is holy." And Joshua did so."* (Joshua 5:13-15, NIV)

The commander of the army of the Lord knows whose side he is on. He is not swayed by who Joshua is, nor who is leading the other army. He doesn't let emotions influence his mindset. He is not impressed by Joshua, his ancestry, his resume, or his position. He is not for Joshua. He is not for the other commander.

He is for the Lord. He knew where he stood. He knew who he trusted. And, what the Lord has commanded him to do in this situation, he will do. He knew his position and that is the position he operated from in all situations.

24) How does knowing where you stand transform your mind to be Kingdom-minded?

_____
_____
_____
_____

25) How does knowing who you trust transform your mind into being Kingdom-minded?

_____
_____
_____
_____

26) How does being for the Lord transform your mind to be Kingdom-minded?

_____
_____
_____
_____

This is another reason why we need the Holy Spirit active in our lives. There are situations we encounter where we think we know God's Will. It's even based on Biblical Truths. However, there are times when God is accomplishing something higher, more important.

God heals in miraculous, mysterious and even so-called natural ways. But He may not want to heal someone at a certain time in a particular set of circumstances. Why? Various reasons.

God's heart is to heal and restore. His more pressing concern is the condition of our hearts and if we're right with Him. He is concerned about our eternity.

I've heard stories of how non-believers have put God to the test and said, "if you heal me, I will follow you." He heals them, they follow Him.

I've heard stories of long-time followers of Christ praying to be healed. They are now face-to-face with the Great Physician.

The point is a Kingdom-mindset seeks God's Will in every situation and trusts Him regardless of the manifested outcome.

We should *always* pray for healing, for by His stripes we are healed. But a Kingdom-mindset seeks and sets their mind on what God wants to accomplish. It may be healing, but a higher perspective may be something else. The Holy Spirit will reveal God's Will to those who seek it out.

A Kingdom-mindset always goes to the Word of God on how to address any situation in their life. It can be incredibly uncomfortable holding yourself to this standard of life. But there is no other way to live if you want to live in true freedom.

27) How often do you go to the Word of God to determine God's Will in a situation?

_____
_____
_____
_____

28) How often to you ask the Holy Spirit what is God's Will in a situation?

_____
_____
_____

29) Are you for the Lord? How is it reflected in your life?

_____
_____
_____
_____

30) How well do you hold yourself up to God's standard of living in Truth, resting in His grace?

_____
_____
_____
_____

> *"So if you're serious about living this new resurrection life with Christ, act like it. Pursue the things over which Christ presides. Don't shuffle along, eyes to the ground, absorbed with the things right in front of you. Look up, and be alert to what is going on around Christ—that's where the action is. See things from his perspective."* (Colossians 3:1-2, THE MESSAGE)

31) What are some steps for you train your mind to be alert to what is going on around Christ?

_____
_____
_____
_____

32) How passionate are you to bring heaven to earth?

_____
_____
_____
_____

33) How do you make embracing the global commission and taking up your personal position a priority in your life?

_____
_____
_____
_____

34) What are some areas of your thinking that do not align with having a Kingdom-mindset?

_____
_____
_____
_____

A person who cultivates a Kingdom-mindset has such a heavenly perspective that they are earthly powerhouses.

35) How do you think you will feel as you and the Holy Spirit transform your mind to be Kingdom-minded?

_____
_____
_____
_____

36) How can continually cultivating a Kingdom-mindset transform:

Your life:_____
_____
_____
_____

Your family: _____
_____
_____
_____

Your friends: _____
_____
_____
_____

Your community: _____
_____
_____
_____

The world: _____
_____
_____
_____

Kingdom-minded people have set their minds on things above, not to dream their lives away. But, to transform this earth according to the Will of God. It is to live as Jesus lived, confronting in love and Truth anything that is not in alignment with heaven.

Become Kingdom-minded and transform this earth for the glory of God and the freedom of others.

Session 6

Made Free Workbook

Yoke of Bondage

"Stand fast therefore in the liberty by which Christ has made us free, and do not be entangled again with a yoke of bondage." (Galatians 5:1)

This session is a long one because it addresses some pretty intense subject matter. Take the time necessary to work with the Holy Spirt on each area. This is about being made free and laying the foundation for the rest of your life. Do not rush through it.

When one begins to embrace the depths of liberty we have been given by Christ, it is at first, joyous, then overwhelming, then, if truly understood, should cause a holy reverence of Almighty God. Why? Because God is, once again, emphasizing the point of personal responsibility for the choices we make. Before you slam this workbook shut, remember, everything flows from God's goodness. He always makes a way! But He always leaves the choice up to you.

Liberty, *freedom from restraint, in a general sense, and applicable to the body, or to the will or mind. The body is at liberty when not confined; the will or mind is at liberty when not checked or controlled. A man enjoys liberty when no physical force operates to restrain his actions or volitions.*

*"...when no physical force operates to **restrain** his, or her, actions or volitions (desires)."*

Jesus has made us free from every yoke of bondage, from every restraint. Every hinderance prohibiting you from living in the promises and blessings of God has been removed through Christ. We are no longer restrained by the demands of the Law, nor by the doctrine man put into place to control people in their relationship with God. Don't forget though, there are still consequences for not choosing godly restraint.

Paul, in Galatians 5, is addressing those who found grace, freedom from the restraints of traditions of men, but have been influenced by someone who told them their righteousness before God still came from the Law. Specifically, you had to be circumcised in order to be accepted by God. They were letting go of grace and picking back up legalism. Legalism is the bondage of works-based relationship, rather than faith-based relationship with God.

"...you who attempt to be justified by the law; you have fallen from grace." Vs. 4b

You cannot earn, pay, or serve your way into God's grace.

"For by grace you have been saved through faith, and that not of yourselves; it is the gift of God, not of

works, lest anyone should boast. (Ephesians 2:8-9)

God, through Jesus Christ, did all the work to set you free from the requirements of the Law, man-made doctrine and even our self-imposed ideas to get our lives whole and healthy. But that does not excuse you from doing a different kind of work.

"For we are His workmanship, created in Christ Jesus for good works, which God prepared beforehand that we should walk in them." (Ephesians 2:10)

We are God's workmanship and we were created to do the good works of the Kingdom. It's being Kingdom-minded. It's a choice, based in love for the Father, to work for Him.

Read Galatians 5.

1) Is there any area of your life you are trying to justify your relationship with God, even validate who you are through "work"? Ask the Holy Spirit to reveal it to you.

_____
_____
_____
_____
_____
_____
_____
_____
_____

2) Works, when not motivated by a faith-based relationship with God, is often an indicator of trying to ease pain, justify an insecurity, self-validation, or an attempt to prove something to another or yourself. Ask the Holy Spirit to reveal any area of your life where these might be a driving factor.

_____
_____
_____
_____
_____
_____
_____
_____

Works-based justification or validation can also creep its way into faith-based good works, such as feeding the homeless, helping orphans, feeding the hungry, even working/serving at a church. But if the driving motivation behind the work is not faith, then it's for naught.

"But without faith it is impossible to please Him, for he who comes to God must believe that He is, and that

He is a rewarder of those who diligently seek Him." (Hebrews 11:6)

Faith comes first. Faith compels us towards good works…for Him. Not to gain validation, security, or acceptance. Faith is what pleases God. Faith should cause us to seek Him.

3) What does God do for those who seek Him? _____

4) Ask the Holy Spirit what it means to be rewarded by God. Write down what He brings to your mind. Do not hesitate, or question, until the Holy Spirit is silent. Then, ask Him more if you'd like.

_____
_____
_____
_____
_____
_____
_____
_____
_____
_____
_____
_____
_____
_____
_____
_____
_____
_____
_____

5) How are we to seek God? _____

Diligent, *constant in effort or exertion to accomplish what is undertaken.*

6) Are you constant in your effort to seek the Lord? _____

> *"For you, brethren, have been called to liberty; only do not use liberty as an opportunity for the flesh, but through love serve one another. For all the law is fulfilled in one word, even in this: "You shall love your neighbor as yourself."* (Galatians 5:13-14)

The restraints have been broken off us by Jesus Christ, we are free. You can choose to use this freedom Christ died to give us for your personal agenda and gain. Or you can choose to use the freedom to live a truly abundant life.

7) What does Paul instruct us to use our freedom for? _____
_____
_____

_____
_____

8) What emotion should be the motivating factor? _____

Paul references, *"all the law is fulfilled in one word"*. If we're no longer restrained by the Law, why does Paul reference the Law? It's because love for us caused God to send Jesus to redeem us. It was love for the Father and love for us that Jesus endured the Cross. It was love that sent the Holy Spirit to us so we would not be alone in this world.

It should be the love for the Father, the Son, and the Holy Spirit that motivates us to love others. Love fulfills the law. If we are in Christ Jesus, then we are compelled to learn how to love God's way.

9) Why do you think it's important to learn how to love God's way? Ask the Holy Spirit.
_____
_____
_____
_____

"But is you bite and devour one another, beware lest you be consumed by another!" (Galatians 5:15)

10) Write down what Paul's warning is saying to you.
_____
_____
_____
_____

Living according to works-based relationships, with God and with others, is exhausting. Even trying to satisfy our own personal desires (flesh) is empty, because without faith in God, we will always have a void in us. It's a burden we were not meant to bear. We, followers of Christ, are meant to live in the Spirit and work by the Spirit. We are to produce Kingdom fruit.

"I say then: Walk in the Spirit, and you shall not fulfill the lust of the flesh. For the flesh lusts against the Spirit, and the Spirit against the flesh; and these are contrary to one another, so that you do not do the things that you wish. But if you are led by the Spirit, you are not under the law." (Galatians 5:16-18)

11) Can you live in the Spirit and in the flesh? _____

Why or why not? _____
_____
_____
_____

> *"Now the works of the flesh are evident, which are: adultery, fornication, uncleanness, lewdness, idolatry, sorcery, hatred, contentions, jealousies, outbursts of wrath, selfish ambitions, dissensions, heresies, envy, murders, drunkenness, revelries, and the like;"* (Galatians 5:19-21a)

12) What are the works of the flesh?

_____
_____
_____
_____

13) What do each of these do to the mind, body and spirit of those who continue to live in them rather than work to bring them under the Spirit?

_____
_____
_____
_____

14) For those who chose to continue to allow them to be active in their lives, including hatred, outbursts of wrath, selfishness, envy, do they inherit the Kingdom of God? _____

> *"...that those who practice such things will **not** inherit the kingdom of God."* (Galatians 5:21b, emphasis added)

It takes faith-based work to remove those from our lives. Paul uses the word "practice" in the above verse. You either practice living by the flesh/law or you practice living by the Spirit.

> *"But the fruit of the Spirit is love, joy, peace, longsuffering, kindness, goodness, faithfulness, gentleness, self-control. Against such there is no law."* (Galatians 5:22-23)

These are the evidence of Christ working in our lives. Galatians 5:24-26 goes on to instruct us that in Christ, we have the ability to eliminate fleshly/temporal desires from our lives. We can live and walk in the Spirit. It's a life worth pursuing, and it's a life unrestrained by works, but restrained by love.

God's commands will always produce life giving results because God set in motion the covenant of reaping and sowing. But this is going to sound odd, His commands will only produce so far if our heart isn't transformed through abiding in relationship with Him, through Christ Jesus.

Legalism, the yoke of bondage, puts work above relationship. Liberty puts relationship above work. When liberty in Christ is first, then relationship drives the desire to do the work God has called us to, internally and externally. Then, and only then, will work not be burdensome.

15) Take an inventory of the Fruit of the Spirit. How evident is the Fruit of the Spirit in your life?

_____
_____
_____
_____
_____
_____

Legalism is one yoke of bondage Christ broke off us. Sin is the other.

Jesus did not eliminate sin from the world. Jesus paid the price so that we, followers of Christ, would not be judged by God under the standard of the Law, but under the standard of grace. Sin is still in the world because God has given us the freewill to choose His way or ours.

Sin angers God because it destroys lives. God sets the standard of what it means to sin, not people. God's standard is the Ten Commandments defined in the Old Testament and they are wrapped up in the two commandments Jesus Christ gave us in the New Testament.

> *"Jesus said to him, "'You shall love the Lord your God with all your heart, with all your soul, and with all your mind.' This is the first and great commandment. And the second is like it: 'You shall love your neighbor as yourself.' On these two commandments hang all the Law and the Prophets."* (Matthew 22:36-40)

16) Why do you think it's possible for all the Law to be contained in these two commandments?

_____
_____
_____
_____
_____
_____
_____
_____

God gave you the freewill to choose, and He will allow you to choose sin.

Always remember, contained within any sin is the seed designed to destroy you. So, think carefully of the choices you make and the impact they have on you and others. God, in His love for you, is relentless in pointing you away from sin and showing you the abundant life found in choosing His ways. But He will not take away your responsibility to decide for yourself.

You are responsible for the choices in your life, and their consequences. It has been this way since Creation. The enemy, who is a very real and cunning adversary, cannot make you sin. He can only tempt you to do so.

*"No temptation has overtaken you except such as is common to man; but God is faithful, who will not allow you to be tempted beyond what you are able, **but with the temptation will also make the way of escape,** that you may be able to bear it."* (1 Corinthians 10:13)

17) After reading 1 Corinthians 10:13, is the excuse, "I just couldn't help myself" a viable excuse to justify choosing to sin? _____

There are standards God calls all followers of Christ to obey. Then there are standards that God individually calls us to that are unique to each person. Disobedience to these unique commands is sin to that specific person.

*"Therefore, to him **who knows to do good** and does not do it, to him it is sin."* (James 4:14)

18) Write down what the Holy Spirit would like to reveal to you regarding this verse. If it's an act of disobedience, ask for forgiveness and what you need to do to realign yourself with God's Will.

_____
_____
_____
_____
_____
_____
_____
_____

Jesus provided the means to receive forgiveness from sin and break the bondage sin holds us in. This does not give us permission to sin! The Father required His Son to pay a brutal price for forgiveness, and for us to abide under grace.

Sin still destroys lives. Empowered by the Holy Spirit you can choose not to sin. But when you fail to attain the standard, which you will you can be set free from its destruction. Repent, ask for forgiveness, move forward and do better. Keep pressing forward.

When you choose not to press forward because of sin, you put to shame what Christ did for you on the Cross. You're telling God, yourself and the world, that the price Jesus Christ paid for grace wasn't enough. There is a heavy price to pay when people choose to wallow in their sin or keep choosing to sin, even though they know better (Hebrews 10:26-31). So, keep moving forward in your relationship with the Father, Son and Holy Spirit.

It's difficult to love when we're dealing with bondage, sin, wounds, fears, insecurities and all those other obstacles life can bring. God is about restoration. He takes us on a journey to restore all that has been lost. He does this, so we can love Him and love others as He hopes.

Generational Sins and Iniquity

There are things in our lives that are handed down through generations. There are beliefs, thought processes, mannerisms, personality traits we develop because of the influence of our family unit and the environment we are exposed to.

There are also sins and iniquity that can run in generations. These can affect us in known and unknown ways. God will deal with these so that you are made free from their influence and the distortions they may cause in your heart and mind.

Generational sins are not just about sinful behavior, it's also about when our hearts are attached to wrong things. They are tendencies and weaknesses passed down from generation to generation.

The Word of God addresses generational sin. It might sound harsh until you understand God was addressing what happens when parents are disobedient, and they pass that disobedience to their children.

> *"You shall not make for yourself a carved image—any likeness of anything that is in heaven above, or that is in the earth beneath, or that is in the water under the earth; you shall not bow down to them nor serve them. For I, the Lord your God, am a jealous God, visiting the iniquity of the fathers upon the children to the third and fourth generations of those who hate Me, but showing mercy to thousands, to those who love Me and keep My commandments."* (Exodus 20:4-6)

The parents created and bowed down to worship false gods. They taught their children to do the same disobedience through words and behaviors. The children, out of habit, chose to do the same thing.

But, when you read the Word of God, EVERY generation was exposed to God's commands. This makes them responsible for their choice to worship God or worship idols. The longer disobedience is allowed in generations, the harder they are to be set free from.

Harder…but not impossible.

So, blaming thoughts, behaviors, and reactions on your parents, family unit, or others who you have been influenced by is a victim-minded excuse. It's not a new creation mindset.

God reveals Himself and the Truth of His commands to EVERY generation.

19) What are some of the things you learned from your parents/guardians (family unit) that are beneficial and healthy?

_____
_____
_____
_____
_____
_____

20) What are some things you learned from your family unit that were not beneficial or healthy?

_____

_____
_____
_____
_____

21) List some thoughts or behaviors or reactions you have that you don't understand why you do them? Ask the Holy Spirit to reveal things to you. For example, I could go from contentment to rage in about 2.9 seconds. I couldn't explain it, and when I thought about it, the reason was trivial. The Holy Spirit revealed the source of the rage and I was able to deal with it. Yes, I still get angry about things, but they are the right things. I can be a healthy, productive angry. It's significantly better than putting my fist through a wall because I couldn't control my emotions.

_____
_____
_____
_____
_____
_____

22) What are some things you may be doing that you know do not align with God's commands? Then, write down why you're doing them.

a. _____

Why: _____

b. _____

Why: _____

c. _____

Why: _____

Generational Iniquity, from *'iwwah, awon, meaning to bend, make crooked,* it expresses *a deviation from the right path.* An iniquity is deeply rooted in us, often formed at such a young age we're not even aware of it.

A generational iniquity bends us towards an incorrect, twisted, stubborn attitude towards self, someone, a people, even God.

>Do you think divorce is an easy option and no big deal?

>Do you think it's acceptable to have sexual relations outside of marriage?

>Do you think getting drunk every Friday night is the way to relax and deal with a rough week?

>Do you think yelling or verbally abusing someone just because they disagree with you is your right?

>Do you think it's no big deal to say degrading things about yourself or others?

>(This is a very short list, and only serves as examples.)

All these thoughts and behaviors could come from you being exposed to them. They've become a part of your belief system without you even realizing it. And, they are a bend towards an incorrect attitude, and they are not in alignment with God's goodness toward you or mankind.

The right attitude towards divorce is not to divorce but to pursue God's design for marriage. The reality is, divorce happens. And there is forgiveness and healing in the wake of divorce. But, again, the right belief regarding marriage is it's a life-long promise. God can restore all things if the people involved are willing to do the work to be restored.

Was your mom absent or critical? Was your father or father-figure abusive? Was the reason for challenging times someone else's fault? Was the phase, "we're broke" used all the time?

Generational Iniquity may include divorce, abuse, sexual sins, sexual perversions and addictions, other types of addictions, rage, prejudice, mental illness, sickness, laziness, poverty, involvement in false religions, criticism, resentment, shame, guilt, passivity, perfectionism and other destructive behaviors and cycles.

All of these, and others, bend us against God's Truth. They are the foundation to which we process all things in life. So, if they are out of alignment with God's Word, He, through His Word and the Holy Spirit will confront them.

23) What are some personality traits you have that you don't like?

a. _____

Why: _____

b. _____

Why: _____

c. _____

Why: _____

24) What are some of your default responses that are not healthy? Or you wish you didn't do.

a. _____

Why: _____

b. _____

Why: _____

c. _____

Why: _____

25) What are some traits you have you don't want to pass onto your children, or even others? Our behaviors are seen by others and can cause them to respond in such a manner.

_____
_____
_____
_____

The Good News is Jesus Christ broke the yoke of generational sins and iniquity at the Cross. If you have done the work to deal with personal sin, yet are still struggling with ungodly thoughts or behaviors, it could be generational sin or iniquity. You have been given the power and authority in Christ Jesus to break generational bondage off yourself and your family line.

Expose the sin. The Holy Spirit will lead you to bring the iniquity into the light of God's glory. Recognize it in yourself and in your family line. It's not about digging deeply into the pain, it's about recognizing the reality of it and holding it up to God's Truth and His glory.

26) Ask the Holy Spirit to reveal any generational sin or iniquity in you or your family line:

_____
_____
_____
_____

Forgive. Forgive those who have caused generational sin and iniquity into yours, theirs and the family line. Remember, this is not about justice for wrongs done. Let God deal with justice. This is about setting you free. Then, it's about setting your family free. This is about stopping the predisposition to wrong things and the damage it does to lives.

"Lord, I forgive _____ for _____. I will no longer hold bitterness or anger towards them. Nor, will I blame them for the thoughts and behaviors in my life that are unhealthy and unpleasing to You. From this day forward, I choose forgiveness, because You first forgave me. I know it will be hard sometimes, but I know You are with me. No longer will the sins of the past influence my future or those who follow me. In Jesus Name, Amen.

Do this for each generational sin or iniquity the Holy Spirit reveals to you.

Repent. We don't always understand what it means to repent. Repent is defined, to feel pain, sorrow, or regret for something done or spoken. It's a grief that we, or others, have grieved the heart of God and we make a conscious choice not to repeat the behavior.

"Lord, I repent of _____. I am so sorry that my thoughts, behaviors and responses haven't been according to Your Word. Holy Spirit, help me to bring every thought captive to the Word of God and to make wise decisions regarding my behaviors. Holy Spirit, help my responses to others glorify God. In Jesus Name, Amen.

Speak Truth. Declare it stops with you! Hebrews 12:27 tells us that those things that can be shaken will be removed. But those that cannot be shaken, they will remain.

"Now this, "Yet once more," indicates the removal of those things that are being shaken, as of things that are made, that the things which cannot be shaken may remain."

Lies are shaken. God's Truth cannot be shaken!

You are free from generational sin and inequity. You need to keep making decisions that align with this freedom.

27) How does this Truth make you feel?

_____
_____
_____
_____

Soul Ties

God created us for relationship. First, with Him, then with others. Relationships were designed to enrich our lives. We were not designed to live life alone. Because of wounds and brokenness, relationships have become unhealthy, and unfortunately destructive.

We seek out, desire, relationships because we are relational in the depths of our being. It's who we are. Because the desire for relationship, to be loved, cared for, not alone is so ingrained in us, we will do almost anything to have relationships, even if it's to our detriment.

Soul ties formed when we bond and attach ourselves to someone or something. There are healthy soul ties designed by God. Then, there are unhealthy ones created by us, and the enemy.

Read the following verses:

> *"And the Lord God said, "It is not good that man should be alone; I will make him a helper comparable to him." (Genesis 2:18)*

> *"And Jesus answered and said to them, "Because of the hardness of your heart he wrote you this precept. But from the beginning of the creation, God 'made them male and female.' 'For this reason a man shall leave his father and mother and be joined to his wife, and the two shall become one flesh'; so then they are no longer two, but one flesh. Therefore what God has joined together, let not man separate." (Mark 10:5-9)*

Luke 1:39-45 is the story of Elizabeth and Mary. It is an example of a healthy soul tie, a healthy friendship. Mary goes to visit her cousin Elizabeth. Both women are pregnant. When Elizabeth heard Mary, the child Elizabeth was carrying leapt. Elizabeth, instead of being jealous, negative, or resentful that her cousin was carrying the Messiah, blessed her! That is a healthy soul tie. It's a healthy relationship.

Read the Book of Ruth (It's short).

Read Samuel 18-20.

28) How are these examples of healthy soul ties, healthy relationships?

29) What are some common traits about these relationships that make them healthy, mutually encouraging?

30) Look at some of the relationships in your life. Identify the healthy ones. Don't discount the relationships the Holy Spirit brings to your mind. Ask Him why He brought them to your mind.

Healthy soul ties do not require relinquishing your personal relationship with God, your identity, worth or purpose. Healthy relationships mutually serve and encourage one another. They respect, honor and love each other. They validate each other's worth. They have healthy, God instructed boundaries.

When we step out of healthy soul ties and enter unhealthy ones, we become fractured. We lose a piece of ourselves. We relinquish pieces of our souls to others or other things. Our souls were meant to belong to the Lord and when any of it has been given to anyone or anything else, there is an emptiness, a void.

The longer we allow that void to grow, the stronger we pursue anything to fill it. The only "thing" that can fill this void, is the love of Father God. Everything else will leave you with an empty pit in your heart.

31) What void are you trying to fill with unhealthy relationships or unhealthy habits? (Sex outside of marriage, over- or under eating, radical exercise, drinking, drugs, prescription or not, etc.)

_____
_____
_____
_____

32) Ask the Holy Spirit to reveal unhealthy soul ties in your life.

_____
_____
_____
_____

Now, break them off by delcaring you no longer have a soul tie with any of the individuals the Holy Spirit revealed to you.

The influence of Social Media has made relationships superficial, unrealistic and fleeting. Social Media relationships create soul ties based on a limited perspective of a person. It creates an atmosphere where fantasy overrides reality.

33) How much do you allow Social Media to influence how you feel about:

God: _____

How does this affect your thoughts and actions?

_____
_____
_____
_____

Yourself: _____

How does this affect how you see and treat yourself? (Does it rob you of your self-worth?)

_____
_____
_____
_____

Your Life: _____

How much dissatisfaction with your life does Social Media create? Does it create ungratefulness for all you do have?

_____
_____
_____
_____

Your Real-Life Relationships: _____

Do you give up real, face-to-face relationships quickly because they require time and effort?

_____
_____
_____
_____

Yes, Social Media can be a soul tie. If you're bound to it more than you are to God, it's a soul tie in your life. If you're identity, self-worth, and validation is linked to the number of likes and shares, it is a soul tie.

If you're engaged on your phone more than the person sitting in front of you....you get the idea.

Read John 4.

34) How did Jesus Christ break off unhealthy soul ties with the woman at the well?

_____
_____
_____
_____
_____
_____
_____

You too can stand in the liberty Christ has given you by breaking off unhealthy soul ties. Ask God to reveal Himself to you as your Father. Renounce, in the name of Jesus Christ, any unhealthy soul tie in your life and take back the entirety of your soul and commit it to the lordship of Jesus Christ. Ask the Holy Spirit to refresh your mind and emotions and restore all that unhealthy soul ties have stolen.

The Flesh

Our own flesh is one of our biggest challenges to overcome in order to live in the liberty of Christ. The flesh can be defined as our own personal and selfish desires/wants that are contrary to the commands of God.

We can be a slave to our flesh and its desires. The world right now is all about doing whatever feels good. This is a reckless and dangerous attitude. The damage this mindset creates is long-lasting and far-reaching. Often the depth of damage these attitudes therefore behaviors are not realized until later in life.

> *"Then, when desire has conceived, it gives birth to sin; and sin, when it is full-grown, brings forth death."* (James 1:15)

35) How do you think *"desire is conceived"*?

_____

36) Write down your thoughts towards sin. Do you think there are degrees of sin? Why or Why not?

37) Now, ask the Holy Spirit about sin. Write down the words that come to your mind.

38) What do you think Scripture is teaching us regarding *"when it is full-grown"*?

39) What does full-grown sin lead to? _____

Identify any area of your life where sin reigns:

We will always battle committing sin. But sin should never have enough power to reign over us. As your relationship with Christ deepens, and you are continually being transformed by His Word, the words, "I just couldn't help it," should never be spoken out of your mouth.

"And those who are Christ's have crucified the flesh with its passions and desires." (Galatians 5:24)

40) Write down what this verse is teaching you:

_____
_____
_____
_____

Controlling the flesh is also about bringing into submission those things that may not technically violate the Word of God, but they still bring you into bondage.

> *"Just because something is technically legal doesn't mean that it's spiritually appropriate. If I went around doing whatever I thought I could get by with, I'd be a slave to my whims."* (1 Corinthians 6:12, THE MESSAGE)

41) Ask the Holy Spirit to reveal to you any area of your life that doesn't technically violate the Word of God but is either hindering you or holding you in bondage. Write it down here.

_____
_____
_____
_____

Ask for forgiveness, repent, and stop doing it. Be made free!

Christ has made us free from the yokes of legalism, generational sin and iniquity, soul ties, and the flesh. Do not be entangled with them anymore.

The Right Kind of Work

God created man(kind) to work, to produce, be fruitful. He never meant for us to be idle. Even in the Garden of Eden, a place of bliss, God prepared a good work for us to walk in.

The work for self-promotion, accolades from man(kind), fortune, any work not motivated by love for God and love for people, will come up lacking. Empty. It will leave us either wanting more of something; or so discouraged we wither away into apathy or nothingness.

The work of God is the work we are to pursue. We were created with a desire to produce, to create something, to bear fruit (be productive). When we co-labor to do the work of the Kingdom, oh what riches and blessings. What joy and belonging!

> *"Therefore we do not lose heart. Even though our outward man is perishing, yet the inward man is being renewed day by day."* (2 Corinthians 4:16)

42) What is the result if we do not lose heart?

_____
_____
_____
_____

43) What is being taught to us regarding our outward man perishing?

_____
_____
_____
_____

44) What does Scripture mean by, *"yet the inward is being renewed day by day"*?

_____
_____
_____
_____

45) Why is *"day by day"* **important?**

_____
_____
_____
_____

> *"But you have not so learned Christ, if indeed you have heard Him and have been taught by Him, as the truth is in Jesus: that you put off, concerning your former conduct, the old man which grows corrupt according to the deceitful lusts, and be renewed in the spirit of your mind, and that you put on the new man which was created according to God, in true righteousness and holiness."* (Ephesians 4:20-24)

46) According to Ephesians 4:20-24, what must we continually put off? _____

47) What is a trait of the former conduct, the old man? _____

48) What is to be renewed? _____

49) Why is this so important? _____

50) Which is who God desires us to be? The old man or the new man? _____

> *"By this we know love, because He laid down His life for us. And we also ought to lay down our lives for the brethren."* (1 John 3:16)

"Now the purpose of the commandment is love from a pure heart, from a good conscience, and from sincere faith," (1 Timothy 1:5)

"Flee also youthful lusts; but pursue righteousness, faith, love, peace with those who call on the Lord out of a pure heart." (2 Timothy 2:22)

"Since you have purified your souls in obeying the truth through the Spirit in sincere love of the brethren, love one another fervently with a pure heart," (1 Peter 1:22)

51) What is the motivating factor in each of these verses? _____

52) Who are we to love? Two of them are easy to see from these verses, but there is a third. Ask the Holy Spirit to reveal them to you _____, _____, _____
_____

In the beginning, it can be challenging to love God and to love others. But the deeper you grow in your relationship with the Father, Son and Holy Spirit, the transformation of your mind and heart makes it easier to love. Love is being poured into you; therefore, love can be poured out.

You must also cultivate a healthy and balanced love of self. You cannot love out of a pure heart, a good conscience, and a sincere faith, if you dislike yourself. I am not speaking to superficial self-dislike. Most of those can be changed through discipline and work.

I am referring to if you carry shame, guilt, wounds which cause resentment and bitterness. Those things we carry within ourselves that make us dread looking in the mirror. God will make you handsome or beautiful from the inside out.

53) Are you able to love from a pure heart, a good conscience and a sincere faith? Write down why.

_____
_____
_____
_____

Change takes work. Healing takes work. Serving the Lord takes work. Loving others takes work. It takes work to produce internal and external fruit. And, it is God's design of us to work and produce…for HIM.

*"I am the true vine, and My Father is the vinedresser. Every branch in Me that does not bear fruit He takes away; and every branch that bears fruit He prunes, **that it may bear more fruit**."* (John 15:1-2, emphasis added)

54) What type of fruit are you producing in your life? Is it beneficial to you, the Lord, others?

"They shall still bear fruit in old age; They shall be fresh and flourishing," (Psalm 92:14)

55) When is it okay to stop working and bearing fruit? _____

"And whatever you do, do it heartily, as to the Lord and not to men, knowing that from the Lord you will receive the reward of the inheritance; for you serve the Lord Christ." (Colossians 3:23-24)

56) According to Colossians 3:23-24, who is all the work we do to be transformed, to make a living, to serve others, for? _____

57) Why is it so important to understand and live this Truth?

58) Write down any other thoughts you have regarding this section.

Session 7

Made Free Workbook

Lies We Believe

*"And the Lord God said to the woman, "What is this you have done?" The woman said, "The serpent deceived me, and I ate." (*Genesis 3:13)

1) Why do you think it is so much easier to believe lies than it is to believe God?

_____
_____
_____
_____

I started this section of the workbook in this manner because trust is foundational in any relationship. We must trust God and His Word above all else. Otherwise, we will continually be tossed about by every word, philosophy, doctrine created by man. If you take a true look at history, everything man has set up, outside of the commands of God, has fallen. It has been proven false.

I am not talking about the things done in the name of God. Mankind has done many things in the name of God, but in reality, it was motivated for the profit of man not the glory of God.

Read Genesis 3.

> *"Then the serpent said to the woman, "You will not surely die. For God knows that in the day you eat of it your eyes will be opened, and you will be like God, knowing good and evil."* (Genesis 3:4-5)

God, in Genesis 2, told Adam not to eat of the Tree of Knowledge. He said that if he did eat, then he would die. The enemy, satan, twisted this Truth and manipulated them into thinking they would be like God. What is so sad, is that they didn't understand they already were. They, and us, are made in His image.

They wanted knowledge, but they weren't prepared for its consequences, even though God told them exactly what would happen. They chose knowledge above relationship.

2) Do you think God wants you to be ignorant? Why or why not? Ignorant is defined as *destitute of knowledge, uninstructed, or uniformed, untaught, or unenlightened.*

_____
_____
_____
_____

3) If God was "afraid" of mankind having knowledge, understanding, why does Scripture say the following:

> *"and He has filled him with the Spirit of God, in wisdom and understanding, in knowledge and all manner of workmanship,"* (Exodus 35:31)

> *"Teach me good judgment and knowledge, For I believe Your commandments."* (Psalm 119:66)

> *"The Spirit of the Lord shall rest upon Him, The Spirit of wisdom and understanding, The Spirit of counsel and might, The Spirit of knowledge and of the fear of the Lord."* (Isaiah 11:2)

> *"for to one is given the word of wisdom through the Spirit, to another the word of knowledge through the same Spirit,"* (1 Corinthians 12:8)

"And though I have the gift of prophecy, and understand all mysteries and all knowledge, and though I have all faith, so that I could remove mountains, but have not love, I am nothing." (1 Corinthians 13:2)

_____
_____
_____
_____

God doesn't have an issue with people having knowledge. He has an issue with the pursuit of knowledge being above a relationship with Him.

Read those verses again. Read them with the recognition that in each of them, knowledge is processed through an understanding of God. Knowledge must be processed and pursued trusting in the One from whom all knowledge comes from. He knows everything. He especially knows you.

4) Write down what comes to mind understanding that knowledge is processed through relationship with Him? Why is this so important?

_____
_____
_____
_____

The essential piece to true knowledge is removed when we take God out of the equation. We are limited in our knowledge and understanding of who He is and who we are when God is not first…especially when dealing with knowledge.

Lies can take root in us through various avenues. Once a lie takes root, it begins to distort reality and we begin to process life through distorted knowledge. Understanding of God, self, and others then becomes distorted because the knowledge we received was faulty. Without God, our worldview becomes inaccurate.

Once we begin to operate out of this place of distortion, wrong thinking, it becomes a stronghold in our lives. God must break down those strongholds, so knowledge and understanding is restored and processed through relationship. Relationship is with the Source, not the knowledge. When knowledge is first, it is an idol.

When we begin to allow knowledge, including what we and others say, exalt itself above who God is and what He says, our lives become unstable. Ultimately, it will end up in chaos, confusion and destruction.

Knowledge, when not rooted in God's Word, takes on a distorted form. It's twisted just enough to make it sound right but isn't quite true.

God never said Adam and Eve couldn't touch the fruit, Eve extended the instructions beyond God's (Genesis 2:17; Genesis 3:3). Or Adam extended God's instructions when he told Eve. Scripture doesn't tell us how the original instructions increased. Regardless, the instructions were shifted from God's original command and created an opening for deception to enter.

5) How often do you take what God says, or others say, and change the narrative? Write down how it changes how you think about things.

_____
_____
_____
_____

The enemy used the same tactic with Jesus in the wilderness (Matthew 4). The enemy used what God said, twisted its meaning, and tried to trick Jesus into choosing knowledge, power, authority above a relationship with God. The difference is Jesus Christ knew He already had all that was important…His relationship with Father God.

What is so amazing is, when Jesus chose God first, God gave Him all the other things…and so much more.

6) What does this tell you regarding trusting God?

_____
_____
_____
_____

We believe lies for a number of reasons. They can become strongholds, incorrect patterns of thinking, in our lives often with us realizing it. We've become accustom to those incorrect, lie based, ways of thinking.

God will deal with them. Always. He deals with them because He must come first. It's not because of His ego. He is completed in who He is. It's because He is our Source for everything, including knowledge. And, it's for our good, at the cost of our ego. We are not complete without Him.

Father / Mother Wounds

Wounds unknowing and knowing inflicted upon us by our fathers, mothers, primary guardians, father/mother figures can run deep.

God created the family unit to be a place of safety, where healthy identities are established, and God-given destinies are nurtured. The breakdown of the family unit has brought deeply seated wounds, insecurities and strongholds of incorrect beliefs of God, self and what life can be.

Father and mother wounds can also occur in the most loving of homes. They should not be discounted because someone had a worse homelife. Any wound needs to be healed and proper thoughts need to be instilled. There is no perfect parent, and it is not dishonoring when parental short comings are acknowledged and forgiven. There is no place for disrespect though.

Depending upon our situation, lies that can come out of father / mother wounds can be: unworthiness; I'm not good enough; I'm a failure; It's my fault my parents (divorced, left me, fight, etc.); I did something wrong, therefore I deserve this abuse; I'm unlovable; I'll never amount to anything; God is like my father, so why would I ever want Him in my life.

Not one of these lies are the Truth of who God is or who He says you are. We must be made free from these lies and replace them with who God says we are. As healing takes place, we grow deeper in our knowledge of God and our knowledge of who we are.

7) Take a moment and think about your relationship with your earthly father (father-figure). Ask the Holy Spirit to reveal to you an area of your life where you were wounded knowingly or unknowingly, by your father.

_____
_____
_____
_____

8) If your father was absent or abandoned you, ask the Holy Spirit to reveal to you how this has impacted how you see God and yourself.

9) This one is not about justice. It's about you receiving healing so YOU can be made free. If you were abused by your father/father figure, write down how it impacted how you see God and yourself?

Healing from father and mother wounds start with you repenting from resentment, bitterness, anger, offense, or unforgiveness you harbor towards your father or mother. It's also about you forgiving them. Yes, it's hard, especially for those who have experienced abuse. But it's not about them. Trust God to deal with them. This is about YOU being made free!

"Lord I forgive _____ for _____ me. I am still _____ (hurt, angry, bitter, even carrying hatred), but I know You are with me. You loved me so much You died for me to receive forgiveness. So, I forgive them. Help me Holy Spirit to truly forgive. I know it might take time, but I know I can so that I will be set free from the lies I've lived because of these wounds. I declare I now live in the freedom Christ gave me. In Jesus Name. Amen."

You may have to pray that often. That is okay. Keep praying it, and it will become a part of who you are…free!

Rejection

The primary root of rejection is the feeling of not be loved or accepted. The good news is we have a heavenly Father and Savior who promises to care for us and will never leave us nor forsake us. But, for us to believe this Truth, we must allow the love and acceptance found in Jesus Christ anchor us. When we are anchored in the love and acceptance of Jesus Christ, rejection, which will happen throughout life, does not lessen our sense of worth.

10) Ask the Holy Spirit to reveal situations in your life where you've experienced rejection. Write them down here.

11) Now, take a moment and forgive the person in those situations who made you feel rejected.

"Lord, I forgive _____ for making me feel rejected, like I wasn't good enough or worth. I release any feeling associated with rejection. I know I will experience rejection from people, in job situations and throughout my life. But, Lord, from this day forward, I will no longer allow rejection to define me. I will no longer believe the lie that I am not worthy. I have been accepted by You and I am loved by You. Holy Spirit, begin healing any incorrect thinking patterns in my life because of rejection. I am worthy and I am good enough because God says so. And no one can take that away from me. In Jesus Name, Amen."

12) Write down any thought the Holy Spirit brings to your mind regarding incorrect thinking patterns established because of rejection. Then, write down a Scripture that replaces that incorrect thinking.

_____
_____
_____
_____
_____
_____

Shame

Shame is an internal narrative we tell ourselves that reinforce the lie we are not good enough. We allow others and ourselves to become our own judge and condemn ourselves to never being good enough.

We hold ourselves up to a standard set by others or ourselves that is based on distorted ideals of what "good enough" is. Standards set by us or others are constantly changing based on cultural shifts, trends, emotions and the ever-elusive—opinions of man(kind).

There is only one standard and it is set by God.

When we violate God's standard, we should feel shame. But it's not the destructive, self-deprecating kind of shame. It's the type of shame where our response is, *"God, I am so sorry I messed up. Please forgive me and help me not to do that again."*

13) Take a moment and ask the Holy Spirit if you are operating from a place of shame in any area of your life. Write it down here.

_____
_____
_____
_____
_____
_____

Now, pray and ask the Lord to forgive you for your mistake and not repenting for that sin when it occurred. Ask the Holy Spirit to remove any distorted thought processes brought on by operating in shame. Then, ask Him to help you replace those distorted thought processes with God's way of thinking.

14) Write down anything that comes to mind as you do the above.

_____
_____
_____
_____
_____
_____

We can also carry shame because of something that has been done to us. We internalize the shame because we think we deserved the action that caused the shame. This type of shame can happen if we're young and are trying to rationalize it because we don't understand what is happening. Or, its spoken to us by the wrongdoer and it takes root in our heart and mind.

I am not justifying the actions of the wrongdoer. This isn't about them. It's about you being made free from lies you've been told, and they hinder your ability see God, yourself, and ultimately others, as God desires.

Do not rush this, get quiet. Ask the Holy Spirit to reveal areas of shame you may be carrying due to the actions of another person. Please keep in mind, some actions that cause shame are unintentional. So, again, this isn't about them, it's about you embracing the freedom found in God's Truth.

15) Write down what the Holy Spirit brings to your memory.

_____
_____
_____
_____
_____
_____
_____

Now, pray:

"Lord, I forgive those who have intentionally and unintentionally caused me to operate in shame. No longer will I allow shame to hold me in darkness and bondage. I will take responsibility for my actions and will be quick to come to You for correction and forgiveness. I will no longer allow the actions of others to create shame in me. I am made free by Your Truths. I will live in Your commands. Shame will not distort your love for me, and it will not distort who You made me to be." In Jesus Name, Amen."

Core Lies

Words are powerful. They can be used to encourage, empower and comfort. They can also be used to cause division, stir up bitterness and create hatred. Words can bring life and they can destroy.

> *"Death and life are in the power of the tongue, and those who love it will eat its fruit."* (Proverbs 18:21)
>
> THE MESSAGE says it this way, *"Words kill, words give life; they're either poison or fruit—you choose."*

Core lies are created as we process through the words and actions of others towards us. The weight the core lie has is in direct correlation to our relationship to the person who planted it and the amount of reinforcement it receives. The reinforcement can be from external factors. And, the reinforcement can come from us if we don't have the security of God's Truth operating in us.

Without God's Truth operating in our lives, we have no defense to come against the lies.

Core lies distort how we see God, ourselves, others and how the world operates around us—they distort and can destroy us just like unhealed Father/Mother wounds and unresolved shames do.

Core lies are in direct opposition to who God is and what He says…about everything.

> Core lie: *"I will always be alone."*
>
> Core Truth: *"I (Jesus) will never leave you nor forsake you."*
>
> Core lie: *"I don't deserve any better."*
>
> Core Truth: *"I (Jesus) have come that they may have life, and that they may have it more abundantly."*

For every lie, there is a Truth that destroys it. But it's up to you to believe the Truth over the lie and live the Truth!

16) Ask the Holy Spirit to reveal any Core Lie you've allowed to operate in your life and write them down:

_____

Take the time to find a Truth that destroys those lies. Write the Truths down so when those lies try to pull you back into its grip, you can quickly speak God's Truth to it. As you do this discipline in this and other situations, the lie deteriorates, and the Truth elevates. This is very important in maintaining your freedom.

I like to use BibleGateway.com. I enter in the word into the search feature and then read the verses until one touches my heart as it pertains to that situation. I know when something (the Holy Spirit) reacts to a verse, I know it's the Holy Spirit telling me that it's the one I need at that time. Then, as I receive greater healing or revelation, He'll bring another verse to my attention.

Inner Vows

Inner vows are the self-preservation promises we make to ourselves in an effort to protect ourselves from pain. They can also be statements we tell ourselves in an attempt to justify not doing something we need to do.

> Inner vows most likely being with, "I will NEVER".
>
> I will NEVER let myself feel like that again.
>
> I will NEVER take a chance again.
>
> I will NEVER let anyone see me hurt/cry again.

Pain, hurt, woundedness, disappointment, failure are all a part of life. The Good News is that God has given us instructions on how we can deal with the challenging side of life without it hindering us from all the amazing things life has to offer.

If you don't let yourself feel, you also diminish the ability to feel joy, peace, hope and love.

Don't allow Inner Vows to isolate you from experiencing the fullness of life.

17) Ask the Holy Spirit to reveal any Inner Vow you have made and write them down:

Repent for making the vow, it doesn't necessarily matter the circumstance. God understands why you did it at the time. But now you know He is your Source; you are not your own source.

Forgive those who have hurt you. Remember, forgiveness is about setting you free. It doesn't mean you have to let those who have hurt you back into your life at this time. God forgave you. You don't have the right to hold

Break your agreement with yourself on how to deal with hurt, pain, wounds. Ask the Lord to become your Healer and Comforter.

Break your alignment with the enemy in dealing with pain. From this moment one, you work through your pain with Almighty God, through the power of His Holy Spirit.

Renounce any agreement that may have been handed to you generationally.

Declare that inner vows and the effects they have had are broken off your life.

18) Write down how you are feeling right now. You will want to remember it when you get discouraged.

_____
_____
_____
_____
_____
_____
_____
_____
_____
_____
_____
_____
_____

Now, for the most important step: ***DEVELOP NEW SCRIPTURE BASED BEHAVIORS!***

You can't keep living how you've been living and expect to live in the freedom God desires for you. Your thoughts, actions and reactions must begin to align themselves with God's Truth and His Commands.

19) Take this moment and get real with God. Talk to Him, ask Him questions about what He thinks about you and then start writing what comes to mind. You will recognize it is His voice because you will have such a sense of peace, grace, kindness, gentleness…even if there is correction and you start crying. In His Presence, there is always peace.

_____
_____
_____
_____

Session 8

Made Free Workbook

Planted

"Blessed is the man who trusts in the Lord, And whose hope is the Lord. For he shall be like a tree planted by the waters, Which spreads out its roots by the river, And will not fear when heat comes; But its leaf will be green, And will not be anxious in the year of drought, Nor will cease from yielding fruit." (Jeremiah 17:7-8)

Planted, *set; fixed; introduced; established.* God desires for you to be planted, to be set, fixed, introduced (brought in), to be established. But you can't be established if you refuse to be planted where God knows you'll flourish at your best.

We live in a transient society. Distance separates family units. We change communities. We transfer in our jobs. We pick up and leave churches. Social media has given us the illusion of community, but it lacks depth of relationship.

1) Think about how many times you've either moved, changed jobs, churches or a like-minded interest group. How did it make you feel pulling up roots and moving to a new location?

_____
_____
_____
_____

2) What was it like for you to build healthy relationships in your new location?

_____
_____
_____
_____

3) How strong, personal, fulfilling are the relationships in the new location? Do you wish they were like the past ones? Why or why not?

_____
_____
_____
_____

The more we change places, the more difficult it can be to establish ourselves and mature because there is little stability in our foundation. The more we remove ourselves from one place to another the more difficult it can become to build healthy relationships because either we aren't as healthy as we should be, or we understand more change is going to come and we want to protect ourselves from pain.

Change is hard. Therefore, we must be planted, set, fixed introduced, established in the Lord first and foremost. This sets the underlying foundation that withstands every other change in our life.

4) How firmly planted do you think you are in trusting the Lord?

_____
_____
_____
_____

Trusting the Lord and putting our hope in Him and His promises gives no room for the excuses of "if only's" and the "when and then" statements. When we are planted in Him, every season of our life is productive, in spite of the circumstances, there is always opportunity for growth and good.

5) List the "if only" excuses you may be telling yourself. Example: "If only I had money." "If only I had a better spouse, job, friends, church." "If only my parents…"

_____
_____
_____
_____

6) Ask the Lord to forgive you for not trusting Him to be bigger than your circumstance. Ask the Holy Spirit to show you want you need to learn and what you need to do regarding each of those excuses.

7) List the "when and then" statements you may be telling yourself. These statements rob you of the joy of the now.

_____
_____
_____
_____

8) Ask the Holy Spirit to help you to embrace the joy, lesson, fulfillment, purpose of where you are right now. Ask Him to help you to trust the Lord with your future, as you are fulfilling the now with excellence.

Do you truly trust the Lord with your life? _____

Do you trust His Word, His promises?_____

Do you truly believe He has your best interests in mind?_____

9) Take a moment and think about your responses. Does your life reflect your answers?

_____
_____

_____
_____
_____
_____
_____

"Blessed is the man who trusts in the Lord, And whose hope is the Lord."

Everything in your life will flow from where you plant yourself. If you want to live a blessed life, you must be planted in Him. A tree can't flourish to its greatest potential if half of its roots are planted in a different pot. Neither can you.

Hope, *a desire of something good, accompanied with at least a slight expectation of obtaining it, or a belief that it is obtainable; confidence in a future event; the highest degree of well-founded expectation of good.* (Webster's 1828 dictionary)

You must plant yourself in Him to Trust for the now and in the Hope of what He says will come.

When our trust is IN Him and our hope is Him, our lives will reflect that of a tree planted by waters.

For a tree to reach its full potential, it must receive the right nutrients. If things are too acidic, too wet, too dry, it hinders the development of the tree. If its roots are damaged, it stunts the growth of the tree, sometimes taking years to recover. In severe cases, parts of the tree die.

The principle is the same for us.

We must be planted, firmly rooted in the things of the Lord. Our relationship with Him is continual so we receive an ever-following stream of nutrients. Our identity is rooted in His Truths and promises. Our mind is fixed on the things of the Lord. Our relationships are based on God's guidelines and our time is spent focusing on His Will.

When you plant yourself in the things of God, applying His commands to your life, you flourish.

"But its leaf will be green" – you will be perpetually growing because you will constantly receive the nutrients you need.

"And will not be anxious in the year of drought," – you're not worried about the seasons of life because you know your Source. Your trust is in Him, the One who sends the rain.

"Nor will cease from yielding fruit," – regardless of the season you're in, you will always be able to produce, to

make a difference, to have meaning and purpose, your life and contribution matter!

Here are some areas where you need to be planted and become firmly established.

>**Practice the presence of God in every area of your life.** God doesn't want just a Sunday relationship. Nor does He want a crisis only relationship. He desires constant communion with each of us.

10) Write down what you think it means to you to practice the presence of God.

_____
_____
_____
_____
_____
_____
_____
_____

11) Now, write down an honest description of practicing God's presence in your life.

_____
_____
_____
_____
_____
_____
_____
_____
_____

12) What changes do you need to make to practice the presence of God in every area of your life?

_____
_____
_____
_____
_____
_____
_____
_____

>**Learn to live as Jesus lived.** Jesus is our aspiration and He is our example. Every excuse we can come up to justify not living this life here on earth as Jesus did when He walked this earth can be overruled by the Word of God.

13) How intentional are you to live your life as Jesus lives His?

14) Jesus held His relationship with the Father above all else. Does your life reflect the same?

15) Do you have the mind of Christ? Are you developing a renewed mind by Christ, or are there areas you allowed to be conformed to the world?

Too often we uproot ourselves from situations and relationships when God hasn't told us to do so and it's not based on Scripture. I am not talking about situations where there is severe mental, emotional and physical abuse, seek out professional assistance in those cases.

I speaking to situations where we pull up our roots, tearing and destroying them because of offense, a sense of injustice, self-centeredness, division, strife, envy, jealousy, self-interest, gossip, and coveting.

When God transitions us, there is grace. When we transition ourselves, there is chaos, confusion, and damaged relationships.

Be Spirit-led. The Holy Spirit is our Teacher, Helper and Comforter. He is the one who leads us to all Truth, God's Truth, and God's Will.

16) How much effort do you invest in knowing the Person of the Holy Spirit?

Be hearers and doers of the Word of God. Hearing the Word of God is not enough. We must also be doers of His Word. We apply His Word, His Commands to our lives and we live it out.

17) How much do you just listen to the Word of God?

___

18) How much of the Word of God do you put into practice in your life?

___

19) When you don't like what the Word of God is telling you to do, what is your response?

___

> **Cultivate the power of prayer.** A healthy, ongoing prayer life is not an option in the life of a follower of Christ.

20) How much time do you spend in prayer?

___

21) Now, how much of that time is spent telling God your list verses just listening to God?

___

> **Fellowship with the brethren (brothers and sisters in Christ).** God is all about relationship, first with Him, then with others. Relationships built with other followers of Christ are mutually beneficial. They strengthen, encourage and support us during times of celebration and times of trials.

God will lead you to a church where you can plant yourself. You'll know when you find the church He wants you to be a part of. It won't be perfect because it's filled with imperfect people. But the church home where you are to be planted will be a place where you worship, fellowship and grow as a person. It's also the place where you will learn to love and serve others.

22) Are you planted in a church where you contribute to its well-being? Why or why not?

23) What are you going to do to be planted deeper in your home church?

24) This is going to sound odd, but I want you to go find a large, healthy, flourishing tree and I want you to describe it here. Example: There are knots and twists on the tree, but it stands strong.

25) Now, I want you to rewrite it here, but replace the nouns and pronouns about the tree with you as the noun and pronoun. Example: There are knots and twists on me, but I still stand strong.

_____

When you think about pulling up roots, read that again and make sure it's God moving you and not you. Being firmly planted in the areas God has for you creates the optimal opportunity for you to reach your God-given potential.

Session 9

Made Free Workbook

Gifted and Positioned by God

"Now concerning Spiritual Gifts, brethren, I do not want you to be ignorant." (1 Corinthians 1:12)

God formed and gifted you with a general and specific purpose in mind. We, in the freewill He has given us, can choose to develop the gifts He has given us to accomplish His purpose, or we can choose to try and forge our own path.

There are gifts, talents, passions, 'natural' abilities God has given you to equip you to live the life you've been given with purpose and fulfillment. The secret to unlock how this is possible isn't a secret; it's usually just an answer we don't like or don't want to do it.

The secret is you do all for the glory of God, not your personal glory, validation, or gain. You maintain a grateful mind and heart for the gifts He has **given you** and you trust the position He **places you** in. Therein is the secret to living in purpose and the contentment we all desire.

> *"And he Himself gave some to be apostles, some prophets, some evangelists, and some pastors and teachers, till we all come to the unity of the faith and of the knowledge of the Son of God, to a perfect man, to the measure of the stature of the fullness of Christ."* (Ephesians 4:11-12)

Ephesians 4:11-12 describes the positions, offices, God has in place to bring structure and balance to His Church. Each of these offices has unique gifting, but the purpose is the same, to:

> *"...come to the unity of the faith AND..."*
>
> *"of the knowledge of the Son of God,..."*
>
> *"to a perfect man..."*
>
> *"to the measure of the stature of the fullness of Christ."*

The offices and the giftings are the diversity. The unity in the team comes from having the same purpose.

1) Make a list of some of the things you enjoy doing. It can be anything, gardening, volunteering, creative things, etc.

_____
_____
_____

2) Think about some of the things you do that make you happy, make you feel good. Don't over think this, there is no wrong answer.

_____
_____
_____
_____

3) What is it about them that make you feel happy, content, or gives you a sense of fulfillment or accomplishment? Then ask the Holy Spirit to reveal how it makes God feel.

_____
_____
_____
_____
_____
_____
_____
_____

Your gifts and talents are meant to be used for the glory of God, and that isn't just inside the walls of the church God has planted you in. You must be planted in a Bible-based, Spirit-led, equipping, world-serving church so your gifts can mature. But that doesn't mean your gifts are confined there.

Your home church is for your equipping and fellowship with other like-minded followers of Christ.

You carry the Kingdom of God with you everywhere you go. And, since most people are not on the staff of a church, this must mean your gifts and positions outside the church walls are to be used for the glory of God, and to be a light to others. You have purpose right where you are currently positioned, and if your heart, mind, and spirit are aligned with God, you will have a sense of fulfillment and accomplishment.

Because you're doing what you are doing for Him above all other motivations!

4) Where are you serving in your home church?

_____
_____
_____
_____

5) Are you embracing all God has for you in your current position?

_____
_____
_____
_____

6) How much time do you spend internally or externally complaining about your current position? Write down why you think that is:

_____
_____
_____
_____

7) How much time do you spend internally or externally complaining about the leadership / direction of your home church? Write down why:

_____
_____
_____
_____

8) How much time to do you spend internally or externally wishing you were doing something someone else is doing? Write down why you think you do that:

_____
_____
_____
_____

9) Where do you currently work? (Stay-at-home moms/dads included)

_____
_____
_____
_____

10) Are you embracing all God has for you in your current position?

_____
_____
_____
_____

11) How much time do you spend internally or externally complaining about your occupation position? Write down why you think that is:

_____
_____
_____
_____

12) How much time do you spend internally or externally complaining about the leadership / direction of your current place of employment? Write down why:

13) How much time to do you spend internally or externally wishing you were doing something someone else is doing? Write down why you think you do that:

14) Read 1 Corinthians 12. Write down four to five take-a-ways you had while reading this chapter.

A few of my favorite take-a-ways are:

- Don't be ignorant of the gifts of God.
- There are different gifts, ministries and activities, but the same Spirit, Lord and God works them all out.
- There are enough gifts to go around.
- There is only one Body and we all are needed, we all contribute, and we all are important to the overall well-being of the entire Body.
- God distributes the gifts as He desires, and He sets the members as He pleases.
- God gives honor to the members, and greater honor to those in the less seen places.

The Gifts of God are not limited to those listed in 1 Corinthians 12—all gifts come from God.

> *"Then the L*ord *spoke to Moses, saying: "See, I have called by name Bezalel the son of Uri, the son of Hur, of the tribe of Judah. And **I have filled him with the Spirit of God, in wisdom, in understanding, in knowledge, and in all manner of workmanship, to design artistic works, to work in gold, in silver, in bronze, in cutting jewels for setting, in carving wood, and to work in all manner of workmanship.** And I, indeed I, have appointed with him Aholiab the son of Ahisamach, of the tribe of Dan; and **I have put wisdom in the hearts of all the gifted artisans, that they may make all that I have commanded you:"*** (Exodus 31:1-6, emphasis added)

The Creator of the Universe is an incredibly creative God. He loves creativity in all of its forms, so long as the creativity is used for His glory, not for motives born out of wounds, bitterness and hatred.

15) Is there a part of your life where you feel stifled—it usually manifests in frustration and anger? Example, I love to write, but my job is primarily in finances. So, with the Holy Spirit, I've learned to embrace my position and to do it with excellence unto the Lord, BUT I've asked Him to help me discipline my time so I can write. Gardening is another favorite pastime, but it doesn't pay the bills, but playing in the dirt brings me peace. So, again, with the help of the Holy Spirit, I discipline my time to enjoy that pastime, because I'm sharing it with the Lord.

16) Where do you feel stifled? What do you enjoy doing but feel like you're unable to do it?

_____
_____
_____
_____
_____
_____
_____
_____
_____

17) What changes in your life do you need to make to align yourself more with the gifting and passions God has given you? This is important to work through because contrary to the world's mantra, you can't do it all. The beauty of that truth is, you weren't meant to.

_____
_____
_____
_____
_____
_____
_____
_____
_____

This doesn't mean you'll do the same thing in the same position all your life. It simply means you can't do all things all at once. You might have to give something up for a period of time. Instead of looking at what you give up, look at what you gain now while you are in route to the future.

Embrace each position the Lord has you in and utilize the gifts He has given you to the fullest. That is where joy, peace, purpose and fulfillment are found. The Holy Spirit is your Teacher, work all things out with Him planted in God's Word.

Begin to Fully Embrace and Operate in Your Gifts

> Pursue the Gift Giver and His Kingdom above pursuing the gifts and position.

18) How balanced are you regarding learning how to do something verses learning about God and His Kingdom?

1 Peter 5:6, *"Therefore humble yourself under the mighty hand of God, that He might exalt you in due time,"*

19) What does this verse tell you regarding promotion in a position?

You need to continually learn to hide your life in Christ.

20) Read John 15:1-8. Write down four Truths about what it means to hide your life in Christ.

21) Now, go back and read John 15:1-8 again. Ask the Holy Spirit to reveal to you what the Lord wants to reveal to you in these verses.

You must be Spirit-led to steward the positions God gives you and the Gifts He equips you with.

22) Why is it so important to listen to the Holy Spirit in correctly operating in the position God has you in?

23) Why is it so important to listen to the Holy Spirit in correctly operating in the gifts God has given you?

24) Put on the Armor of God. (This is covered in the next chapter) Read Ephesians 6:10-18. Write down why the Armor of God is necessary for followers of Christ to have.

25) Do not neglect the gift(s) that is in you. Read 1 Timothy 4:13-15. Ask the Holy Spirit why it is important not to neglect the gifts God has given us. What do you think happens when we do neglect the gifts?

26) Read 1 Corinthians 12 and 1 Corinthians 14:12. Write down what these Scriptures tell us regarding the purpose of the Gifts.

27) Who positions in the Body and Who is the gift-giver? _____

Why is this so important to keep in mind? What perspective does it give you regarding your gifts?

28) What does God say about the positions and gifts who are hidden (behind the scenes)?

29) Read 1 Corinthians 13:1-3. What should motivate the use of every Gift?

30) How effective are we in the position God has us in, or the Gift He has given us, if we don't operate in them from this motivation?

_____
_____

There are excellent resources to help you identify and learn about your Spiritual Gift(s). Make sure you include the Holy Spirit in your pursuit of maturing in the Gifts of God. Below are several Spiritual Gifts with their corresponding Scripture reference. I encourage you to study them and pursue those the Holy Spirit leads you to, then learn about the other ones.

- Word of wisdom (1 Corinthians 12:8; Luke 6:9)

- Word of knowledge (1 Corinthians 12:8; Luke 18:22)

- Faith (1 Corinthians 12:9; Acts 3:6)

- Gifts of healing (1 Corinthians 12:9, 28; Acts 28:1-10)

- Working of miracles (1 Corinthians 12:10; Acts 6:8)

- Prophecy (1 Corinthians 12:10; 1 Thessalonians 5:20-21; Ephesians 4:11)

- Discerning of spirits (1 Corinthians 12:10; Luke 8:29)

- Tongues (1 Corinthians 12:10, 28; Acts 19:6)

- Interpretation of tongues (1 Corinthians 12:10; 14:13-33)

- Helping (1 Corinthians 12:28)

- Administration (1 Corinthians 12:28; Acts 6:2-3)

- Ministry/service (Romans 12:7; 2 Timothy 1:16-18)

- Teaching (Romans 12:7; Ephesians 4:11-14)

- Encouragement (Rom. 12:8; Hebrews 10:24-25)

- Giving (Romans 12:8; 1 Corinthians 13:3; Acts 4:32-35)

- Leadership (Romans 12:8; Acts 13:12)

- Mercy (Romans 12:8; Luke 5:12-13)

- Apostleship (Ephesians 4:11)

- Evangelism (Ephesians 4:11; 2 Tim. 4:5)

- Pastoral guidance/Shephard (Ephesians 4:11)

- Grace (Romans 12:6; Ephesians 3:7; 4:7; 1 Peter 4:10-11)

- Willingness to face martyrdom (1 Corinthians 13:3)

Intercession (Romans 8:26-27)

Hospitality (1 Peter 4:9)

Celibacy (1 Corinthians 7:8)

Don't forget, God gives other gifts too. Are you skilled with your hands? Good with numbers? Love writing stories? Good with music? Crafts? Every good and every perfect gift is from above, from God Himself.

31) Write a few things down that you're good at. This isn't pride, it simply is. It becomes pride when your identity and validation come from it. So, keep up with those heart checks.

_____
_____
_____
_____
_____
_____

32) Read Galatians 5:22-23. Write down what should be evident in your life.

_____
_____
_____
_____
_____
_____

33) Read 1 Corinthians 13:112-3. Where are we to abide regardless of the gift or position?

_____
_____
_____
_____
_____
_____

34) What is the greatest one? _____

Serve well…but love better!

Session 10

Made Free Workbook

Weapons of Our Warfare

"For though we walk in the flesh, we do not war according to the flesh."

(2 Corinthians 10:3)

We are in a war…which has been won by Christ Jesus. But battles still rage on. Battles will continue to be waged until the return of Jesus Christ. The prize of every battle is the hearts, minds and souls of people from the perspective of eternity.

God's motivation is the love He has for humanity. His heart is for people to choose to spend eternity with Him and every tear will be wiped away, there will be no more death, nor sorrow, nor crying. There will be no more pain.

The enemy's motivation is fueled by unimaginable pride, jealousy and an intense hatred of God. The enemy, satan, only comes to steal, kill and destroy. He deceives many away from God through lies and preying upon their pain, insecurities and fears. He cares nothing for them; he only wants to destroy them to "hurt" God.

But God, through His amazing love, made a way for us to not only spend eternity with Him, but gives us the tools to live this life in abundance. His name is Jesus Christ and He is the Way, the Truth and the Life. And, our relationship with Father God, Jesus Christ and the Holy Spirit are our greatest weapons in every battle we face.

1) How does knowing that there is a battle going on for your heart, mind and soul make you evaluate how you live your life?

_____
_____
_____
_____

2) How much belief do you put into that satan wants to destroy your life because of his hatred of God and all God has created? Why?

_____
_____
_____
_____

The life you have been given is not happenstance. There is no such thing as coincidence. Life is a series of actions and reactions. Choices and consequences. One is with you to continually guide you towards Life. The other is continually trying to pull you towards death.

You are the one who chooses which path you take. And, you are the one who chooses how many people you take with you.

3) How does knowing this Truth change how you see your life and your life's influence on others?

_____
_____
_____
_____

> *"For though we walk in the flesh, we do not war according to the flesh. For the weapons of our warfare are not carnal but mighty in God for pulling down strongholds, casting down arguments and every high thing that exalts itself against the knowledge of God, bringing every thought into captivity to the obedience of Christ, and being ready to punish all disobedience when your obedience is fulfilled."* (2 Corinthians 10:3-6)

The battleground is in our hearts and our minds and it's for our souls.

4) Why is knowing where the battle takes place so important? Read 2 Corinthians 10:3-6 again.

_____
_____
_____
_____

The entry points are the eyes and the ears.

5) Why is knowing the entry points to the battlegrounds so important? Read 2 Corinthians 10:3-6 again.

_____
_____
_____
_____

To win the battle before it begins you are careful of what you let in through what you see and what you hear. Then, you take every thought captive and you hold it up the Truth of God's Word.

If it is in opposition to the Heart, Will and Word of God, you get that thought out of your mind. It's not enough just to try and not think about it, you must replace it with a promise of God.

6) Why do you think it's so important to replace wrong thoughts with a promise of God?

_____
_____
_____

The enemy cannot make people do anything. The enemy can only tempt (which is your flesh, your internal desires) or influence through subtle deception, manipulation, or outright lies.

However, I will warn you right here, when you play with the occult (witchcraft), you give the enemy and his minions greater access to your mind and will. They will have greater influence over you and possession is a real thing. They will use you and then when you are of no further use, they will destroy you. The spirit realm is real. It's not a playground to be dabbled in, toyed with or be double-minded about. You must learn and abide in the authority and power of Jesus Christ.

7) If the enemy cannot make people DO anything, and God can't tempt you to sin, who's responsible for the choices they make?

___
___
___
___

> *"Blessed is the man who endures temptation; for when he has been approved, he will receive the crown of life which the Lord has promised to those who love Him. Let no one say when he is tempted, "I am tempted by God"; for God cannot be tempted by evil, nor does He Himself tempt anyone. But each one is tempted when he is drawn away by his own desires and enticed."* (James 1:12-14)

8) What is the reward when you win the battle over temptation?

___
___
___
___

You must know the Word of God and live in His commands, His ways, to be made free and live in true freedom. The Word of God contains the weapons you need to overcome every adversity you face.

Read Ephesians 6.

9) Read verses 6-4 – Pray about them for a moment. Write down what the Holy Spirit is telling you about these verses. It might be a difficult thing, but its important. For example, how do you honor a father or a mother who has been neglectful, absent or even abusive?

Honoring your father and mother is a command of the Lord. It's not optional. But you have to receive healing from the Lord to be able to do so. Honoring your parents is about your freedom first, then it opens the opportunity for them to be healed by the Lord (their choice and responsibility, not yours). You will also learn that honoring doesn't require putting yourself in harm's way.

If you don't honor your parents using the wisdom of the Holy Spirit, a battle is lost. And, a portion of your freedom is still in chains. I will say it again, honoring your parents does not mean putting yourself in harm's way. You can honor your parents by not hanging onto anger, bitterness, offense, disappointment—thinking and speaking ill of them.

___

Read verses 5-9.

10) How do you apply these verses to today? Write down four spiritual Truths about these verses and how they apply to your life now? How can they bring your freedom?

___

Read verse 10.

11) Who are we to be strong in? _____

Read verse 11.

12) How much of the armor are we supposed to put on?

___

13) What do you think happens when we only put on part of the armor of God on?

___

14) What and who are we standing against?

___

Read verse 12

15) Who do we wrestle against?

_____; _____; _____;
_____

16) Who are we not wrestling against?

_____
_____
_____
_____

17) Why is this important to keep in mind who we are really fighting?

_____
_____
_____
_____

Read verse 13.

18) Again, how much of the armor are we supposed to put on? Why?

_____
_____
_____
_____

19) What are we withstanding?

_____
_____
_____
_____

20) When we have the full armor on, what is our stance?

_____
_____
_____
_____

Stand, *to remain fixed, not to yield, not to fly; to maintain the ground; to persist in opposition or resistance; not to yield or comply; not to give way or recede.* (Webster's 1828 Dictionary)

21) What does it mean to you when Paul tells us, "…and having done all, *to stand*"?

_____
_____
_____
_____

Read verses 14-15.

22) Write down how God's Word instructs us to stand?

_____
_____
_____
_____

God's Truth in the innermost parts of our being keeps us steady and secure.

God's righteousness is a shelter and protection for our heart, so we can love God and love people well.

The Gospel of peace protects our feet (path) because we carry the peace of God with us.

Read verse 16.

23) Why do you think Paul says, *"above all"*, when referring to the shield of faith?

_____
_____
_____
_____

24) What is the purpose of the shield of faith in this verse?

_____
_____
_____
_____

Read verse 17.

25) What is the purpose of the helmet of salvation?

_____
_____
_____

26) The sword of the Spirit represents the Word of God. Given this, how important do you think it is for you to know and live Scripture?

_____
_____
_____
_____

27) If you don't know Scripture, how effective do you think you'll be in battle?

_____
_____
_____
_____

Read verse 18.

28) How often should we pray? _____

29) What type of prayers should we be praying?

_____
_____
_____
_____

> *"For if I pray in a tongue, my spirit prays, but my understanding is unfruitful. What is the conclusion then? I will pray with the spirit, and I will also pray with the understanding. I will sing with the spirit, and I will also sing with the understanding."* (1 Corinthians 14:14-15)

30) According to 1 Corinthians 14:14-15, is there only one way to pray? _____

31) Verse 18 tells us to be watchful. What does being watchful to you mean? What are you to be watchful for?

_____
_____
_____
_____
_____
_____
_____

> *"Therefore humble yourselves under the mighty hand of God, that He may exalt you in due time, casting all your care upon Him, for He cares for you.*

Be sober, be vigilant; because your adversary the devil walks about like a roaring lion, seeking whom he may devour. Resist him, steadfast in the faith, knowing that the same sufferings are experienced by your brotherhood in the world. But may the God of all grace, who called us to His eternal glory by Christ Jesus, after you have suffered a while, perfect, establish, strengthen, and settle you." (1 Peter 5:6-10)

32) How is being humble a weapon of our warfare?

_____
_____
_____
_____

33) What does being sober and vigilant mean to you? How vigilant are you about your life?

_____
_____
_____
_____

34) Why do we need to be vigilant?

_____
_____
_____
_____

35) Who is the adversary seeking to devour?

_____
_____
_____
_____

36) Why is resisting him such a powerful weapon?

_____
_____
_____
_____

37) What are we to remain steadfast in?

_____
_____
_____
_____

"Therefore submit to God. Resist the devil and he will flee from you. Draw near to God and He will draw

near to you. Cleanse your hands, you sinners; and purify your hearts, you double-minded. Lament and mourn and weep! Let your laughter be turned to mourning and your joy to gloom. Humble yourselves in the sight of the Lord, and He will lift you up." (James 4:7-10)

38) Who do we submit to?

_____
_____
_____
_____

39) Who do we resist?

_____
_____
_____
_____

40) Who draws near to us when we draw near?

_____
_____
_____
_____

41) Who lifts us up?

_____
_____
_____
_____

The greatest weapon you have is your relationship with Father God, through Jesus Christ. The Holy Spirit teaches you how to stand your ground in the power and the authority of Jesus Christ. In order to stand, we must humble ourselves and trust God in the midst. He has given us the victory of the war and He has given us the weapons to win each battle.

The last One standing wins, and His desire is for you to be standing beside Him.

Chapter 11

Made Free Workbook

Prayer is Not Optional

"For this reason we also, since the day we heard it, do not cease to pray for you, and to ask that you may be filled with the knowledge of His will in all wisdom and spiritual understanding;" (Colossians 1:9)

The importance, power, and effectiveness of prayer is evident throughout Scripture. There is story after story of how people prayed, individually and corporately, and God moved on their behalf in miraculous ways. Scripture records that Jesus Christ Himself would often go off alone to pray. If Jesus, the Son of God, prayed, how much more should we?

Prayer at its most intimate is having an open and honest conversation with God. Prayer at is most powerful changes the destinies of people and nations. A healthy, continual, effective prayer life is essential to a follower of Christ. Prayer is not optional.

In Paul's letter to the Colossians, he tells them that his unceasing prayer for them are that they, *"be filled with the knowledge of His (God's) Will in all wisdom and spiritual understanding."* That is a pretty powerful prayer.

1 Thessalonians 5:16-18 tell us to: *"rejoice always, pray without ceasing, and in everything give thanks."* In everything, not just the good times. Prayer is about relationship. God wants you to hunger for it, the enemy wants to do everything to keep you from it.

Why? Because God uses the vehicle of prayer to co-labor with us to bring heaven to earth. The enemy knows if he can keep you from prayer, you are not a threat to his agenda to steal, kill and destroy lives.

1) How active is your prayer life? Why?

_____
_____
_____
_____

2) How fulfilling is your prayer life? Why?

_____
_____
_____
_____

3) What are three challenges you have in cultivating a healthy, purposeful effective prayer life?

_____
_____
_____
_____

4) How much does your prayer life increase during a crisis?

_____
_____
_____
_____

Prayer is the conduit that activates the Truth and Will of God in your life. You are meant to have a meaningful and intimate private prayer life that manifests in a powerful contribution to corporate prayer.

Personal Prayer

> *"But you, when you pray, go into your room, and when you have shut your door, pray to your Father who is in the secret place; and your Father who sees in secret will reward you openly. And when you pray, do not use vain repetitions as the heathen do. For they think that they will be heard for their many words."* (Matthew 6:6-7)

5) Why do you think Jesus instructed us to pray privately?

_____
_____
_____
_____

6) Who is in the secret place? _____

7) Why do you think that God is found in the secret place when He is omnipresent?

_____
_____
_____
_____

8) How does God reward when our private prayer life is meaningful?

_____
_____
_____

9) What do you think Jesus means when he says *"…do not use vain repetitions"*? **Is He saying to only pray about something once?**

_____
_____
_____
_____

10) What do think is the heart issue behind Jesus' statement, *"for they think they will be heard for their many words"*?

_____
_____
_____
_____

Prayer is personal. Therefore, you need to pray as the Holy Spirit teaches you how to pray, with your personality. Because prayer is not about just the words, prayer is about the heart.

Jesus did give us a model prayer. We could pray it every day and nothing ever happens if our heart and faith isn't in it…again, it's about relationship. The prayer Jesus teaches us in Matthew 6 provides guidelines, a protocol, on maintaining the proper perspective and heart in prayer.

"Our Father in heaven, Hallowed be Your name."

Hallowed means holy. God's name, His being, His nature is holy. He is above all and He is to be revered, worshipped and praise above all.

Our prayers should reflect this Truth. Yes, He wants us to walk and talk with Him. He wants to be in relationship with us. But our familiarity in our relationship with Him should never dishonor, take for granted, or disrespect Him. He is God.

11) How do your prayers honor and respect God?

_____
_____
_____
_____

"Your kingdom come."

Jesus teaches that we are to pray for God's Kingdom to come to earth. One, that means it's possible, two, it means we should never stop praying for His Kingdom to come to earth.

12) How often do you pray for God's Kingdom to come to earth? Why?

_____
_____
_____
_____

"Your will be done on earth as it is in heaven."

We are to pray for God's Will to be done here on earth as it is in heaven. In order for us to know what that is, we need to study Scripture about what God's Will is so when we see something that isn't in alignment with it, we know we can pray that situation to be changed for God's Will.

13) How often do you pray for God's Will to be done verses your will to be done? Why?

_____
_____
_____
_____

"Give us day by day our daily bread."

God not only will help us take care of our physical needs, but spiritual needs as well. Jesus is called the Bread of Life, and in Deuteronomy 8:3 we are taught that, *"man shall not live on bread alone but on EVERY word that comes from the mouth of God."* We need daily nourishment from the Word of God.

14) List four ways you can receive spiritual nourishment for your soul:

a. _____

b. _____

c. _____

d. _____

15) Are you prioritizing spiritual nourishment in your life? Why or why not?

_____
_____
_____
_____

"And forgive us our sins, For we also forgive everyone who is indebted to us."

Jesus died for our sins. We still need to ask for forgiveness a lot, because we still sin, a lot. We are also called to forgive others. We might not like it, but we are instructed to forgive others. God, through Jesus Christ, has forgiven us. Withholding forgiveness harms us, impedes our prayers, and sometimes hinders others from receiving healing.

16) Do you take the time in your prayer life to confess, repent and receive forgiveness for your sins? Why or why not?

___

17) How committed are you to forgiving others, regardless of what they may have done to you? Remember, forgiveness isn't about putting yourself in harm's way. It is about releasing God's promises in your life.

___

"And do not lead us into temptation, But deliver us from the evil one."

God doesn't lead us into temptation, our selfishness, covetness and fleshly desires do. This is acknowledging our weaknesses to Him and entreating His help to lead us away from them. He always provides a way out of temptation. It's our decision whether we take it or not.

18) How honest are you with God about the temptations you face?

___

Evil is in the world. We need God's continual guidance, power and authority to deal with it. The enemy was defeated at the Cross by Jesus Christ. Yet, he is still in the world and it is still his intention to destroy as many as he can.

19) Do your prayers reflect our reliance on God to deliver us from evil?

___

"For Yours is the kingdom and the power and the glory forever. Amen."

20) How well do your prayers convey that it is God's Kingdom that has the power and receives the glory?

_____
_____
_____
_____

Nurture a personal prayer life. It is a cornerstone of a life in Christ. A personal prayer life unlocks the keys of heaven.

Corporate Prayer

Followers of Jesus Christ are meant to fellowship and do life together. This means, we hear, study and live the Word together. We worship together. We serve the church and the community together. And, it means we pray together.

21) When you meet with other followers of Jesus Christ, how much time is spent in prayer together? Why?

_____
_____
_____
_____

Corporate prayer is simply followers of Christ coming together to seek out the Word of the Lord and His Will. Prayer should be done decently and in an orderly fashion (1 Corinthians 14:40). This means there should be a leader, not a dictator.

A leader guides the group through prayer, usually with topics they believe the Lord is leading them to pray about. They facilitate the group so there is order, and order doesn't mean control. But it does mean that when someone, either out of a lack of understanding, immaturity, or a need to be heard speaks up and is out of order, they are gently, and lovingly, corrected. Not humiliated. However, there have been times when I've had to strongly correct someone in corporate prayer because they refused to be in order. They either refused to let others be heard, or they tried to take control and turn prayer in a different direction. This is rebellion, usually because they need validation due to a wound not being healed and identity not being restored by Jesus Christ.

22) Have you been in corporate prayer times when you've witnessed something happening that "just didn't feel right"? Yes / No

23) If yes, how was it handled and how did you handle it?

_____
_____
_____
_____

I've been in a corporate prayer setting and I sensed something that just didn't seem right. So, I put my arms around the friends I came with and I prayed over myself and over them. There are times when the Holy Spirit leads you to confront incorrect things outwardly (but rarely in a way that publicly humiliates another person) (Matthew 18:15-17). And there are times to cover yourself and let the Holy Spirit deal with the situation.

There is much controversy when speaking in tongues in a corporate setting. The Bible is clear about how speaking in tongues is facilitated in 1 Corinthians 14:26-33. Study it for yourself so you'll understand when speaking in tongues is in order and when its out of order.

Because 1 Corinthians 14:34 has been misrepresented about women speaking in church, I want to address it here. Paul was addressing a lack of understanding and giving instruction so things in a corporate setting would be done decently in order. Women were talking and asking questions instead of listening. They were being disruptive because they didn't understand. It's the same as if Joel Osteen or Joyce Bridges were speaking and someone, man or woman, jumped up and asked a question. It isn't the time or the place for a disruption or distraction like that to occur.

Read 1 Corinthians 14:26-33.

24) How many "out-loud" prayers should be offered in tongues during corporate prayer? _____
_____
_____

25) What other gift should be in operation when tongues are used "out-loud"?
_____
_____

26) What should those praying in tongues do when the other spiritual gift is not being operated in?
_____
_____
_____

27) When you pray in tongues, what is its predominate use? (Jude 20, Romans 8:26, Romans 8:27)
_____
_____
_____

Other Types of Prayer

There are many types of prayer, but there is only one purpose…to grow closer to God and be used of Him to bring forth His Will. Prayer is about transforming ourselves into all God created us to be and to mature in our relationship with Him. Maturity allows us to be entrusted with the power and authority He delegates to us to accomplish His

Will here on earth.

28) I'm going to list the various types of prayers with a corresponding verse to read. Write down what each type of prayer means to you based on these Scriptures.

The Prayer of Confession (Psalm 51:2-3, 1 John 1:9)

_____
_____
_____

The Prayer of Commitment (1 Peter 5:7)

_____
_____
_____

The Prayer of Listening (Isaiah 40:31, Psalm 27:14, 1 Kings 19:13)

_____
_____
_____

The Prayer of Fellowship (1 Thessalonians 5:16-18)

_____
_____
_____

The Prayer of Thanksgiving (1 Thessalonians 5:18, Psalm 100:4)

_____
_____
_____
_____

The Prayer of Praise (Exodus 15:2)

_____
_____
_____

The Prayer of Worship (Psalm 95:6)

_____
_____
_____

The Prayer of Scripture (Knowing God's will and praying it)

The Prayer of Agreement (Matthew 18:19-20)

The Prayer of Intercession (Numbers 14:11-21; Ezekiel 22:30)

The Prayer of Request or Supplication (Matthew 7:7-12; John 14:12-14; Luke 1:13)

The Prayer of the Prophetic (2 Peter 1:19-21, 1 Corinthians 14:1-3; 1 Timothy 4:14)

The Prayer of Praying in Tongues (1 Corinthians 14:1-3; 1 Corinthians 14:17-19)

The Prayer of Warfare (Mark 9:17-29; Acts 19:11-20; Ephesians 6:12)

The Prayers of Praying for One's Enemies (Matthew 5:43-45)

To be Made Free and to live free requires cultivate a healthy, ongoing, ever deepening prayer life. It is not optional if you want to live the overcoming abundant life Christ has given you access to.

> *"Be anxious for nothing, but **in everything** by prayer and supplication, **with thanksgiving,** let your requests be made known to God; and the peace of God, which surpasses all understanding, will guard your hearts and minds through Christ Jesus."* (Philippians 4:6-7, emphasis added)

Chapter 12

Made Free Workbook

Pressing Toward the Goal

"I press toward the goal for the prize of the upward call of God in Christ Jesus." (Philippians 3:14)

Press toward the goal! Yes! Let's go! I'm ready! Hum, what is the goal? The goal is to pursue everything God has for you in Christ Jesus. Reaching out to Jesus Christ and become all He desires us to become and accomplish all He has for us to accomplish. To celebrate each other as we achieve success, to weep with each other when we experience pain, to encourage each other when we encounter challenges.

I love THE MESSAGE version of Philippians 3:12-21.

> *"12-14 I'm not saying that I have this all together, that I have it made. But I am well on my way, reaching out for Christ, who has so wondrously reached out for me. Friends, don't get me wrong: By no means do I count myself an expert in all of this, but I've got my eye on the goal, where God is beckoning us onward—to Jesus. I'm off and running, and I'm not turning back."*
>
> *15-16 So let's keep focused on that goal, those of us who want everything God has for us. If any of you have something else in mind, something less than total commitment, God will clear your blurred vision—you'll see it yet! Now that we're on the right track, let's stay on it.*
>
> *17-19 Stick with me, friends. Keep track of those you see running this same course, headed for this same goal. There are many out there taking other paths, choosing other goals, and trying to get you to go along with them. I've warned you of them many times; sadly, I'm having to do it again. All they want is easy street. They hate Christ's Cross. But easy street is a dead-end street. Those who live there make their bellies their gods; belches are their praise; all they can think of is their appetites.*
>
> *20-21 But there's far more to life for us. We're citizens of high heaven! We're waiting the arrival of the Savior, the Master, Jesus Christ, who will transform our earthy bodies into glorious bodies like his own. He'll make us beautiful and whole with the same powerful skill by which he is putting everything as it should be, under and around him."*

Read verses 12-14.

1) Do you have to have everything figured out before you start on this journey?

_____
_____
_____

2) What about in the middle of this journey? How important is it to have everything figured out?

_____

3) What do you think is more important to God, perfection or progress?

4) Who is the goal and how does that apply to you?

5) Who is beckoning us to the goal and why do you think that is?

6) Are you walking/running forward, or do you keep looking back?

7) If you're looking back, what are you looking back on and why? How do you get past it and move forward into what God is beckoning you towards?

Read verses 15-16

8) What is all of our goal?

9) What can blur our vision? Who can clear it if we let Him?

_____
_____
_____

10) What is the right track?

_____
_____
_____

Read verses 17-19.

11) Who are we to stick with in our race toward Christ? Who do we keep track of in this race?

_____
_____
_____
_____
_____
_____

12) Who do we need to watch out for, be on guard against so we don't get off track? Why is this important to keep in mind?

_____
_____
_____
_____
_____
_____

There are, for lack of a better word, common goals every follower of Christ is to pursue. Goals such as, but not limited to:

- A personal relationship with Father God, through Jesus Christ.
- Being transformed by the renewing of our minds so we prove the good, and acceptable and perfect Will of God.
- Cultivating the fruit of the Holy Spirit in our lives, love, joy, peace, longsuffering, kindness, goodness, faithfulness, gentleness and self-control.
- Worshipping the Lord individually and corporately.
- Praying individually and corporately.
- Be a generous person through our giving, time, talents and gifts.
- Overcoming evil with good.
- Live out the greatest commandments of Loving God and Loving People.
- Fulfilling the Great Commission.

"And Jesus came and spoke to them, saying, "All authority has been given to Me in heaven and on earth. Go therefore and make disciples of all the nations, baptizing them in the name of the Father and of the Son

and of the Holy Spirit, teaching them to observe all things that I have commanded you; and lo, I am with you always, even to the end of the age." Amen.

Every single person who professes Jesus Christ as their Lord and Savior has a purpose in fulfilling the Great Commission. Your purpose is to help fulfill the Great Commission in whatever position, capacity, sphere of influence, gift, talent, economic status, education level, you are in.

A stay at home mom has just as much importance in doing her part as an evangelist does in doing theirs. That stay at home mom may be training up a child who may become the leader of a nation who turns that nation back to Christ.

13) What are you currently doing to fulfill the Great Commission?

_____
_____
_____

14) What can you do in your current situation to fulfill the Great Commission more effectively?

_____
_____
_____

15) What do you dream about doing that would contribute to fulfilling the Great Commission?

_____
_____
_____

Our lives should be a continual testimony to the Truth, faithfulness and promises of God. Our lives should reflect the Truth that once we were lost and now we are saved. We have a hope and a future. We have overcome by the Blood of Jesus Christ, the word of our testimony and not loving our lives so much we weren't willing to lay them down for Him.

We can't do everything. But all of us can do something. That is the beauty of the Body of Christ and how God designed and positioned us to work together.

You matter and your part matters, for your good and God's glory!

You have been MADE FREE by the goodness of God. Not perfect, but free. You owe it to God and someone else to help them find the same freedom through a personal relationship with Jesus Christ as you have. There is no Greater Purpose.

16) Write down five things you can do right now to fulfill the Great Commission.

1) _____
2) _____
3) _____
4) _____
5) _____

Remember, God never told Joshua to be like Moses. He said He would be with Joshua like He was with Moses. God told Joshua that He would never leave him nor forsake him. So, don't try to be a Joel Osteen, Priscilla Shirer, Beth Moore, TD Jakes, or Joyce Meyer, each of these amazing men and women have pursued what God has asked of them. You need to pursue what God has for you!

God is with you. He will never leave you nor forsake you. He desires for you to be the best you ever and to walk in the works He prepared for you…but you can't do that if you're trying to be someone else.

Keep your eyes on Jesus, the Author and Finisher of your faith.

Run your race!

Part 3

Made Free Workbook

Final Encouragement

"The thief does not come EXCEPT to steal, and to kill, and to destroy. I have come that they may have life, AND THAT THEY MAY HAVE IT MORE ABUNDANTLY." (John 10:10, emphasis added)

You have one life to live. You have a loving Heavenly Father who has moved mountains to give you the opportunity to live life now in freedom and live eternally with Him in peace and joy. You also have an enemy whose sole objective is to rob you of joy now and for all eternity. That is His one goal, to destroy you.

Jesus Christ defeated the enemy with the work at the Cross. He came so that not only you could have life, but that you would have it more abundantly. THE MESSAGE versions says it like this: *"I came so they can have real and eternal life, more and better life than they EVER DREAMED OF."*

You will have challenges. You will have difficult seasons. Jesus told us we would have trials and tribulations here in this world. But He also said to be of good cheer for He has overcome the world.

The promises of God are yes and they are AMEN. His way leads to life. His Truths will refine and transform you. He has a hope and a future for you. He prepared good works for you to accomplish. If He is for you, who can stop you!

Press on towards the prize. Finish this race well. Keep your eyes on Jesus Christ for He will direct your path.

Embrace A Life Lived In Freedom!

With Joy,

Your sister in Christ,

Tracy Edwards

Acknowledgments

My life is a result of the graciousness and the faithfulness of the God I serve. He has never given up on me, even when I gave up on Him and myself. My life is a testimony to the love of God and the Truth of His promise to bring beauty from ashes. Father God, thank You for all You are. To my two fathers in Heaven, thank you for loving me. To my mom Paula and my mom Eva, thank you for always believing in me. To my husband, children and grandchildren, I am rich because of you. My wonderfully steadfast friends who stand by me, call, text, or email at just the right moment, hold me accountable and keep encouraging me to finish this race well, I love you beyond words. To the Prayer Partners and Missions Team at Freedom Church, Carrollton, Texas, it's a joy to advance the Kingdom of God with you. To the Freedom Church Family, it's an honor to do life with you. I am truly blessed beyond measure!

Keep being Made Free for the glory of God!

About the Author

Tracy L Edwards was born and raised in south Texas. She grew up in the country raising show animals and riding horses at rodeos. She married her husband Steve in 1995 and they have three children and two grandchildren. She enjoys reading, writing, trying to grow plants, going on adventures with her family, and working with her husband on their land. Her passion is to see people experience the love of God and fulfill the purpose they were born for. Her heart is to see people live in the hope, peace and joy that is available through the truth found in a personal relationship with Jesus Christ.

She loves to speak, teach and equip others to embrace a life lived with purpose and passion.

You can contact her at:

Email: up-word@outlook.com

Website: Up-WordBound.com

www.ingramcontent.com/pod-product-compliance
Lightning Source LLC
Chambersburg PA
CBHW081230080526
44587CB00022B/3879